LIVING FOR ETERNITY

Life With Eternal Rewards In Mind

Matthew Robert Payne

Living for Eternity

More information about Matthew can be found at
http://www.matthewrobertpayneministries.net

Matthew also can be found on Facebook in a group that he runs called "Open Heavens and Intimacy with Jesus." that can be found here https://www.facebook.com/groups/OpenHeavensGroup/

Matthew has written several other books before this one and they can be found on his Amazon author page here

http://www.amazon.com/Matthew-Robert-Payne/e/B008N9R896/ref=ntt_athr_dp_pel_1

Editor Melanie Cardano from www.upwork.com

The opinions expressed by the author are not necessarily those of Revival Waves of Glory Books & Publishing.

Revival Waves of Glory Books & Publishing
PO Box 596
Litchfield, IL 62056
United States of America
www.revivalwavesofgloryministries.com

Revival Waves of Glory Books & Publishing is committed to excellence in the publishing industry.

Published in the United States of America

Ebook: 978-3-9592-6822-6

Paperback: 978-0692520284

Hardcover: 978-1-62676-999-1

DEDICATION

This book is dedicated to every person trying to work out their reason for living. It is my prayer that this book will challenge you and inspire you to live a life that is more focussed on external rewards.

I dedicate this book to the Holy Spirit. Have your way Lord!

ACKNOWLEDGEMENTS

June Payne

I thank my mother for copy editing this book and adding her wisdom and she went. It is a better book for it. My mother is a great mother, full of love, encouragement and great editing skills.

Melanie Cardano

I want to thank Melanie for proof-reading the book and working hard on it for me. I want to thank Melanie for her continuing friendship. Melanie can copy edit, or proofread your book and can be hired as a freelance worker at www.upwork.com

Bill Vincent

I want to thank Bill Vincent of Revival Waves of Glory Books and Publishing for preparing this book and getting it to the marketplace.

Holy Spirit

Thank you for helping me write this book and helping my mother to copy edit it.

Jesus and Father

Thank you for loving me and giving my life direction and purpose. You can never be repaid by me. I pray my life will continue to bring You both glory.

Table of Contents

Chapter 1
WHAT IS ETERNITY?

"I have seen the God-given task with which the sons of men are to be occupied. He has made everything beautiful in its time. Also, He has put eternity in their hearts, except that no one can find out the work that God does from beginning to end. I know that nothing is better for them than to rejoice and to do good in their lives, and also that every man should eat and drink and enjoy the good of all his labour - it is the gift of God." Ecclesiastes 3:10-13

The overall theme of the Book of Ecclesiastes can be summed up in the question asked in Chapter One, verse three: *"What profit has a man from all his labor in which he toils under the sun?* This is like saying: "What's the meaning of life? Surely, there must be more to it than just existing for a short time and then dying?" Most people at some stage ponder this.

God created a physical world in which we are all born into. However, no matter how we spend our life here on earth, we will all spend eternity in one of two places: either in Heaven or in Hell. This book is going to have its focus on living our life on earth in such a way that we will be assured of eternal life in Heaven. There are many books that talk about Hell but this book is not going to be one of them.

In the opening passage in Ecclesiastes 3:10-13, Solomon assures us that each of us has had eternity placed in our hearts by God Himself. This means that we all instinctively know that this life on earth is not all that there is to live. However, many people deny what is naturally in them. They say instead, that we are on earth to live our life and when we die, our existence will cease.

This type of person will probably also deny the existence of God. However, most of us realize that there *is an existence beyond this life.* Therefore, the hereafter should have an impact in what we do here on earth. We should all strive to live a life that will make a "positive" impact in this world, and that will introduce us to a better life that is to come.

Solomon says that we cannot know the works of God from beginning to end. Suffice to say that God is God, and He has always been. However, through Jesus, His Son, we can get to personally know God, and be directed by Him in this life. God lives in eternity and He alone knows our future in every detail. Therefore, if we are going to live for eternity, it makes sense that we should take the time to really know God. We need to learn how to walk in a way that brings pleasure to our Creator, whilst we live our relatively short time on earth.

What is our eternal life going to be like? How can we possibly understand it?

For a believer, eternity will reach its highest point in Heaven, where we will be continually happy because we will be totally fulfilled in learning and growing in glory. Heaven is outside of time, but all of earth's past, present and future believers will live in this timeless paradise and we will be continually growing in wisdom and in the things of God.

In direct contrast, eternity in "Hell" will be a place of everlasting torment that was originally created for the devil and his demons. Hell is not a place than any of us would want to go to, yet Jesus said in Matthew 7:13 that many people are travelling on the road to destruction.

Eternity in "Heaven" is a place where God and man cooperate perfectly. It is a place where perfection in life is a constant, living reality. It's an everlasting paradise where God will have His children absolutely delighted in who they were created to be, since the foundation of the earth. In eternity, we will all live in our destined purpose and everyone will bless each other as they go about their everyday life in Heaven; forever and ever.

Receiving "eternal life" is not something that we should put off till we get to Heaven. We can be certain of this because when Jesus was interceding to His Father for us, the night before He went to the cross, He said to His Father: *"And this is eternal life, that they may know You, the only true God, and Jesus Christ whom You have sent." John 17:3*

Therefore, at salvation, we entered into eternal life because *knowing Jesus is eternal life.* Later, in the Epistle of John, this truth is reinforced: *"And this is the testimony; that God has given us eternal life and this life is in His Son." 1 John 5:11*

Again, in the epistle of John, we read: *"He who believes in the Son of God has the witness in himself; he who does not believe God had made Him a liar, because he has not believed the testimony that God has given of His Son." 1 John 5:10*

Knowing about Jesus is not enough; eternal life is having a personal relationship with Jesus, the Son of God. HE IS eternal life and He is the only One who can take us to His Father's home in Heaven. Jesus said: *"I am the way, the truth, and the life. No one comes to the Father except through Me."John 14:6.* Those who have asked Jesus to be their Savior already have "Eternal Life" residing in them, so they are already Heaven bound. For the believer, this wonderful miracle occurred.

We don't "earn" salvation by good works. The Bible tells us that we can only receive salvation by faith in the finished work of Christ Jesus on the Cross. *"For by grace you have been saved through faith, and that not of yourselves; it is the gift of God, not of works, lest anyone should boast." Ephesians 2:8-9.* Salvation comes from faith in God's work, not ours.

This verse tells us that salvation is a totally-underserved gift that God, in His grace, extends to all those who, by faith, humbly believe and receive Jesus as their personal Savior. We are to recognize that God even supplies the faith to believe. We can never therefore earn salvation, no matter how many good works we do. Works, too often puff us up with personal "pride" and this, together with self-centeredness, is the basis of all sin. Therefore, God is not impressed by anyone boasting about themself or their works. In fact, the Bible warns us that *"God resists the proud, but gives grace to the humble." James 4:6.*

Once we receive God's gift of salvation and His Holy Spirit enters our human spirit, we will discover that we will naturally do good works as a result of God's presence within us. Good works, therefore, are the *result* of personal salvation; they are never the cause of it.

Christianity is all about man having a personal *relationship* with God. Religion, on the other hand, is man, by self-effort, trying to reach up to a holy God. This is absolutely impossible, yet all the major religions of the world are based upon earning "merit" with the Creator God. If this were at all possible, God the Father had no need to send His Son to die for us.

Christianity is all about what God has done for us and our faith response to *His work alone.* God took the initiative to reach down to us, for we could never reach up to Him. Our part is to respond by faith in Christ alone and give glory to the Holy Spirit who has patiently been working behind the scenes in our life, bringing us to the point where we cry out for help. Good works on our part will be the natural fruit of salvation, because of our love relationship with our Creator God.

In times past and even today, there are billions of people who deny the Lordship of Jesus Christ, but God's Word assures us that one day in the future, everyone ever born will acknowledge that Jesus Christ is Lord. However, when this event occurs, it will be too late to receive salvation because the time of God's grace will have passed. The clock is ticking down towards that day. None of us can be sure of having a tomorrow. If you are reading this book and you are not sure whether you will go to Heaven, then it is time that you speak to a mature Christian whom you respect, and ask them to lead you to Christ. *"Behold, now is the accepted time; behold now is the day of salvation." 2 Corinthians 6:2b.*

*"Your attitude should be the kind that was shown us by Jesus Christ, who though He was God, did not demand and cling to His rights as God, but laid aside His mighty power and glory, taking the disguise of a slave and becoming like men. And he humbled Himself even further, going so far as actually to die a criminal's death on a cross. Yet it was because of this that God raised Him up to the heights of Heaven and gave Him a name which is above every other name. That at the name of Jesus every knee shall bow in Heaven and on earth and under the earth, and every tongue shall confess that Jesus Christ is Lord, to the glory of God the Father." * Philippians 2:5-11 (Living New Testament)

We are to surrender our life to Jesus before we die, because physical death does not end conscious existence. We have been warned that after death, we will face a judgement: *"it is appointed for men to die once, but after this the judgment." Hebrew 9:27.* Some people believe in reincarnation but this is the devil's lie. The Psalmist confirmed this: *"We are but "a breath that passes away and does not come again." Psalm 78:39b*

Man was originally created in the image of God. (Genesis 1:26) Therefore, like God, we are eternal beings. Our quest is to make sure that we spend our eternity with God and not separated from Him forever. God loves all of us, even those who are presently far away from Him. In fact, God *"desires all men to be saved and to come to the knowledge of the truth, for there is one God and one Mediator between God and men, the Man Christ Jesus who gave Himself a ransom for all." 1Timothy 2:4-6.* Knowing Jesus is the only way to Heaven.

When we live our lives with "eternity" in mind, we will think and react very differently about almost everything. Far too often, we worry about things that have no eternal value at all. By recognizing this, we can save ourselves from useless worry. With these things in mind, I hope that I can motivate my readers to become excited about their faith in Jesus, so that they will start living and planning their life with eternity in mind; right now on earth.

Strictly speaking, eternity is without beginning or end, like the existence of God. However, Christians have God Himself indwelling their human spirit. The things in this book will relate to all those who have been granted eternal life through Jesus Christ, our Lord. In my experiences with God the Father and Jesus, I have come to know much about Heaven and what we can expect to find there. But before we get there, we have a life to live down here on earth. To successfully live that life, we need to have purpose and a sense of destiny in what we do. Living aimlessly with no directional purpose is not a fulfilling life, in fact, it can be the very opposite.

King Solomon, in my opening verse in Ecclesiastes, exhorts us, as sons of men, to be busy and to labor in life, as he implies that this is what is going to bring us lasting fulfilment. He says that our life and our ability to work is God's "gift" to us. Therefore, it makes sense for us to be actively pursuing what we were created to do. Many of us have personally discovered that life is far more rewarding if we work. However, life can be even more satisfying if we work with a concept of building up treasures in Heaven. It is this eternal perspective that will be addressed in this book.

As Christians, there are many things that God has called us to do. For example: We are to be joyful always; to pray without ceasing; to give thanks in all situations; to forgive others; to go the extra mile; to exhibit the fruit of the Holy Spirit and be ambassadors for Christ. In fact, we are to love others as we love ourselves and to love the Lord with all our heart and soul. In the process of doing all these things, God will cause us to discover His "personal work" for us to do.

I am a simple man. I have no theological certificates. Whilst we explore the coming chapters, I will be writing out of my knowledge and current beliefs. Life has taught me many things; the Holy Spirit has taught me many things; and other gifted speakers have added to my understanding. However, I pray that you enjoy simplicity and you are not turned off that this book will not be a major theological text. While some chapters have numerous Bible quotes, others may not have any. It depends on where the Holy Spirit leads me in each chapter.

CHAPTER 2
WHY IS ETERNITY IMPORTANT?

Jesus warned the church in the last chapter of the Bible: *"Behold, I am coming quickly, and My reward is with Me, to give to everyone according to his work." Revelation 22:12.*

At first glance, this verse may seem to be somewhat confusing because Ephesians 2: 8-9 quite clearly says that it's our "faith" not our works that God is interested in. Salvation is based solely on our belief "in the finished work of God" through Jesus His Son, on the Cross.

However, if you are looking at the Bible through the lens of "eternal" rewards, you will discover that all believers are going to be rewarded in Heaven according to "their works" on earth. It's important for us to know that "all these works" will be works that we have done *since becoming a Christian.*

In summary: we can't get to Heaven by our works, but we will get to Heaven, if by faith, we put our trust in the finished work of Jesus. However, once we arrive in Heaven, our eternal "rewards" will be determined by the works done by us, *since believing in Jesus.*

I have discovered that some people resist the subject of eternal rewards. Perhaps, they don't like the idea of some people in Heaven having a more rewarding experience than others. We can, however, readily determine in the Gospels that Jesus was against us storing up futile "earthly" treasures. He said: *"Do not lay up for yourselves treasures on earth, where moth and rust destroy and where thieves break in and steal; but lay up for yourselves treasures in Heaven, where neither moth nor rust destroys and where thieves do not break in and steal. For where your treasure is, there your heart will be also." Matthew 6:19-21*

Jesus wants us to chase after His eternal Kingdom treasures. We are to enjoy things, but we are not to love these things; we are to love only people and God. We are to know that God is not against us having luxuries if we can afford them, but He is opposed to material things controlling us. It's a tragedy when people begin to trust in their material goods instead of trusting in God, who has provided them in the first place by gifting man to work and create.

Always bear in mind that earthly treasures are only temporal, whilst Heavenly treasures are eternal. God wants us to enjoy our possessions, but He detests selfish and extravagant materialism that ties a person to the mindset of the world. Besides, we can't take any physical thing with us when we die, so what is the use of storing something, without the hope of redeeming it at some later stage?

> We learn from Scripture that the church is the New Testament "temple" of God. *"Do you not know that your body is the temple of the Holy Spirit who is in you, whom you have from God, and you are not your own? For you were bought at a price; therefore glorify God in your body and in your spirit, which are God's."* 1 Corinthians 6:19-20

Because we represent God's temple, we are not to do or say things that may cause schisms in the body of Christ, but we are to build on the firm foundation of Christ Jesus. Paul said: *"Why do you judge your brother? Or why do you show contempt for your brother? For we shall all stand before the judgment seat of Christ." Romans 14:10.*

Each person is responsible to God and the right of such judgment has been given to Christ. *"For the Father judges no one, but has committed all judgment to the Son." John 5:22.* For a brief time, Jesus was God veiled in human flesh. He was the God-Man: fully God and fully man. Jesus can testify what it's like being confined to a human body with its fleshly weaknesses and limitations. Jesus purchased our redemption with His Own blood. Being full of wisdom, justice and mercy and always obedient to His Father's will, He has truly earned the right to be God's appointed Judge of the world.

Weak and strong Christians alike shall all individually stand before the Judgment Seat of Christ. There will be no unbelievers present, for this judgment will determine the degrees of reward we will each enjoy in Heaven, according to our "works" as a believer. Some people call it the Bema Judgment Seat because the word "Bema" denotes a raised platform, where athletes receive their medals. This was the practice in early Athens. Today, we use a similar Bema at the Olympic Games for our current champions to receive their medals.

This judgement is not to be confused with the "Day of Judgment" where, at a much later date, there will be a vast company of people standing guilty before the Lord. This awesome Day will be very sombre as it will be the reckoning day for "unbelievers only" since the time of Adam and Eve. The souls and spirits of those who have died will be raised from their resting place and all living unbelievers on earth at that time will attend this judgment.

> Now, back to believers. Paul has told us: *"For we are God's fellow workers; you are God's field, you are God's building. According to the grace of God which was given to me, as a wise master builder I have laid the foundation, and another builds on it. But let each one take heed how he builds on it. For no other foundation can anyone lay than that which is laid, which is Jesus Christ."* 1 Corinthians 3:9-11

All believers make up God's "worldwide church" – known as "His living temple." Jesus Christ is the Chief Cornerstone of this living temple. Therefore, ministers of the Gospel are to be wise builders and shepherds, as they are ultimately responsible to God alone. As leaders, they are to teach their flock sound doctrine based on the sure foundation of the Lord Jesus Christ. Long before Christ, King Solomon built God a glorious and extravagant temple, but after the death and resurrection of Jesus, we learn that *"the Most High does not dwell in temples made with hands" Acts 7:48.* Now, God dwells in living "human" temples.

Some Christians may be ignorant about Heavenly rewards, but the Bible teaches that Jesus will judge the individual works of every believer since they were saved. By having a sound doctrine which leads to a closer walk with God and a deep love for others, a believer's works will hopefully be classified as being gold, silver or precious stones. If this is the case, their works will survive the test of fire and they will receive *many* eternal rewards in Heaven.

Now if anyone builds on this foundation with gold, silver, precious stones, wood, hay straw, each one's work will become clear; for the Day will declare it, because it will be revealed by fire; and the fire will test each one's work, of what sort it is. If anyone's work which he has built on, endures, he will receive a reward. If anyone's work is burned, he will suffer loss; but he himself will be saved, yet so as through fire. " 1 Corinthians 3: 12-15

In contrast, some believers compromise the truth of God's Word; they are careless in their walk with God and are bad witnesses to the goodness and holiness of God. The "works" of these believers will be classified as "wood, hay or straw" and will quickly burn up in God's test in Heaven. Though they suffer eternal loss of reward, they will still enter Heaven because of the indwelling Holy Spirit residing in them.

Perhaps, the main reason why people don't give eternal rewards much thought is that they haven't had teaching on the subject. I want you to know that living in the light of eternity will definitely have its rewards at this Judgment Seat of Christ because the decisions made that day by the Lord will be irrevocable.

On that judgment day, you will be given your Heavenly

position and assignment, based on the knowledge you have of God, the doctrines you live by, your faithfulness to your gifting and the opportunities God has given you since your salvation. Decisions made by the Lord will be eternal decisions, which will result in the type of work you will enjoy in Heaven.

If our present life is just all about us, we need to change our attitude, as self-centeredness will not result in many Heavenly rewards. Our present life is only for a season, whereas eternity is forever. A child only has short-term vision, but a child of God is to have long-range vision.

Jesus spoke much about the importance of living a life of self denial. When Peter said to Jesus: *"You are the Christ, the Son of the living God"* in Matthew 16:16, Jesus replied: *"Blessed are you Simon Bar-Jonah, for flesh and blood has not revealed this to you but My Father who is in Heaven. And I also say to you that you are Peter, and on this rock I will build My church, and the gates of Hades shall not prevail against it."* Matthew 16:17-18.

Note: Jesus instantly gave His disciple a name-change. But most importantly, Jesus called Peter's revelation a rock. This "rock or revelation truth" is absolutely pivotal in becoming part of God's family. In reality, every believer since that time has received the same revelation from God and that is: *Jesus Christ is God's anointed One – Jesus Christ is God!*

The Jews had long been waiting for their promised Messiah to come and save them from their enemies; the word Messiah means God's anointed One. In fact, most Jews today are still waiting for their Messiah to come and save them from their enemies, because they don't realize that their forefathers insisted that He be put on a cross, over two thousand years ago.

Immediately after Peter's revelation, Jesus began to explain to His disciples that He was going to suffer and be killed. Although Peter believed that Jesus was the long awaited Jewish Messiah, he vehemently rejected the idea that suffering and death would come to God's anointed. Jesus rebuked him and said: "*If anyone desires to come after Me, let him deny himself, and take up his cross, and follow Me. For whoever desires to save his life will lose it, but whoever loses his life for My sake will find it. For what profit is it to a man if he gains the whole world, and loses his own soul? Or what will a man give in exchange for his soul?*" Matthew 16:24-26

Today, this type of message is not very often preached from the pulpit. It would certainly not be a popular sermon to say to people that they needed to deny themselves on earth so as to gain Heavenly rewards. The very idea of self-denial is abhorrent to most people.

What does self-denial actually look like? Who preaches this kind of stuff? Surely, being a Christian who regularly attends church and does their best to obey God is enough. After all, Jesus died for our sins, isn't that enough? Why should Jesus need us to carry a cross? And if we were to consider carrying a cross, what would our cross look like?

Self-denial can be doing something different with your time and resources than what other people do. Self-denial can be living in such a way that others are blessed and not all your time and resources are spent on personal wants and desires. Self-denial differs from person to person. Self denial can't be said in a one-size-fits-all sort of way. For example: to a mother who lives at a rubbish tip in one of the slums of the world, self denial would look different to the executive who earns eighty thousand dollars or more each year.

My Testimony: Many years of my life were lived in personal pain because of an addiction. It took a long time for me to become free of that habit, but when I did became free, I was used to spending so much money each week on my sin and now I had spare cash each week. Jesus introduced me to self denial by encouraging me to give my money to beggars each week - two dollars at a time.

19

For many years, I paid my bills and simply gave away all my spare cash.

However, in the last three years, Jesus has led me to write books and self-publish them. The self-publishing process takes a lot of money and nearly every pension day has two hundred dollars going towards my latest project. I do this because I see my books as "Kingdom seed" that will be sown into the lives of people. I willingly choose to deny myself of unessential things in order that I might sow into producing books, so that people will grow in the Lord.

I delight to serve the Lord. I love to see how many of my books have been downloaded. I particularly get excited every time I make them free. I am excited each time I release a new book and start to read the reviews of the book as people read them and bless me with their feedback in the public forum on Amazon. I love people to write to me and tell me what impact one of my books had on them. I am fulfilled in life and excited on my journey with the Lord.

I urge you to consider whether there is something you could deny yourself in order to direct money or even your talent or time into something beneficial for Kingdom purposes. I pray that you will seriously consider these things and move from simply existing in this world, to prospering in every single way in your life.

Considering eternity is very important, it's where you are going to live forever! In eternity, you will live with either "little reward" or you will live with "great" reward. The Bible assures us that *what we do with our life on earth, will determine these future things.* None of us wants to see our works burn up at the Judgement Seat of Christ, so that we are left with little or no rewards for all eternity. On that day, we will desperately want to hear our Master say to us: *"Well done, good and faithful servant; you were faithful over a few things, I will make you ruler over many things. Enter into the joy of your lord." Matthew 25:25*

We need to prepare for eternity. Yes, we know that all

believers will live in Heaven one day, but not all of them will share identical fulfilment. I urge you to consider these things in order to make your future life far more rewarding. After all, your time in Heaven will be eternal.

Understand that the amount of enjoyment accounted to you in Heaven will be determined by how you choose to live your life now on earth. You may choose to live a life here on earth without denying yourself anything. You may only have short-term vision and want to just live for today's pleasures. So many Pastors in different churches are always preaching on prosperity and living in abundance here on earth. (They can't be wrong, surely?)

So far, we have been told that we should deny ourselves and take up our cross; our earthly works will be tested by fire; and that this test will determine our rewards for all eternity. When Jesus told us to take up our cross and follow Him, we need to personalize for ourselves what our particular "cross" looks like, as it will vary according to our life and circumstance.

My Testimony: Each person's cross can be different. Sometimes, the Holy Spirit has me write things that are hard for me to write, but He has an eternal purpose that is bigger than me. For instance, sharing that I had an addiction for many years was something that the Holy Spirit had me share. It might not have been needed for most people to find that out, however, there are some readers who may be encouraged that I had a debilitating sin-life for many years even whilst being a Christian and that by the grace of God, I overcome it. Obeying the Holy Spirit and sharing that for the greater good is a way 'I take up my cross' in writing.

There are many small and bigger crosses that the Lord has me to carry. Each of them will have a significant purpose because God is good, all the time! I am content to be a simple person, who is trying to do God's will each day and this, I know, brings glory to Him.

The thing that is huge about "eternity" is that it's a long, long, time; it simply never ends.

Some believers say that we will arrive in Heaven with all knowledge but I think if we haven't spiritually grown much on earth, we will arrive in that state and our spiritual knowledge will then be rapidly accelerated. This "acceleration" seems to be confirmed in Scripture. *"For now we see in a mirror, dimly, but then face to face. Now I know in part, but then I shall know just as I also am known." I Corinthians 13:12*

I believe that we will go on learning more and more in Heaven; our appetite for knowledge will supernaturally increase. I also believe that if we have lived in a supernatural way on earth, we will see things even more supernatural when we arrive in Heaven.

Jesus revealed His true identity to his disciples, and later in the same chapter, He stressed the importance of self-denial, He then said: *"For the Son of Man will come in the glory of His Father with His angels, and then He will reward each according to his works."* He also prophesied: *"Assuredly, I say to you, there are some standing here who shall not taste death till they see the Son of Man coming in His kingdom." Matthew 16:27-28.*

What did Jesus mean by that closing statement? Six days later, in the presence of His three closest friends, Peter, James and John, Jesus was supernaturally and gloriously transfigured before them: *"His face shone like the sun, and His clothes became as white as the light and behold, Moses and Elijah appeared to them, talking with Him." Matthew 17:1-3*

While He was still speaking, behold, a bright cloud overshadowed them; and suddenly a voice came out of the cloud, saying, "This is My beloved Son in whom I am well pleased. Hear Him!" Matthew 17:5. Just like Peter, James and John, God the Father wants us today to take notice of the words of Jesus.

That day, these three disciples actually saw their Master in all

His glory. History has confirmed that many times, prophecy in Scripture can have a former and latter fulfilment. We are told that one day, Jesus will again majestically shine like the sun in the clouds. On this wonderful and awesome Day, Jesus will supernaturally draw up from the earth all those who belong to Him.

Like many Christians before me, I can't help but wonder if the prophecy in Matthew 16:28, when Jesus told His disciples: *"Assuredly, I say to you, there are some standing here who shall not taste death till they see the Son of Man coming in His kingdom"* will be again true in this generation. I wonder whether we will be the privileged generation who will see Jesus majestically coming with His great cloud of witnesses to supernaturally collect us from earth as described below:

> *"For the Lord Himself will descend from Heaven with a shout, with the voice of an archangel, and with the trumpet of God. And the dead in Christ will rise first. Then we who are alive and remain shall be caught up together with them in the clouds to meet the Lord in the air. And thus we shall always be with the Lord."* 1 Thessalonians 4:16-17

> *"Behold, I tell you a mystery: We shall not all sleep, but we shall all be changed – in a moment, in the twinkling of an eye, at the last trumpet. For the trumpet will sound, and the dead will be raised incorruptible, and we shall be changed."* 1 Corinthians 15:51-52.

Whenever this event happens, it certainly makes sense to live a life today with eternity in mind, investing our time, talents and resources into doing God's "Kingdom" business rather than foolishly wasting our lives chasing after things on earth that have no eternal value.

CHAPTER 3
WHAT IS HEAVEN LIKE?

"Eye has not seen, nor ear heard, nor have entered into the heart of man the things which God has prepared for those who love Him." 1 Corinthians 2:9

These days, there seems to be a multitude of books about Heaven. Yet, it's hard to find a book on Heaven that is full of revelation. The best books I have read so far are by Kat Kerr called, "Revealing Heaven 1" and "Revealing Heaven 2." Kat has been on trips to Heaven over a thousand times and has far more experience about it than anyone else that I know of. I would suggest that you purchase her books and read for yourself the great hope that Christians have.

I have had many conversations with the Lord about my eternal destiny and I've been to Heaven quite a few times in visions and dreams. If I thought that I could write a better book on the subject than Kat Kerr has done, I would ask the Holy Spirit to help me write it.

As you read this, you might not have heard of those two books, so I will cover some of what I personally know about Heaven. Of course, this is only a little glimpse and I stress, a far more comprehensive look can be found in Kat Kerr's writings and videos on YouTube.

Heaven is much like earth, but far bigger and more exciting. Heaven is always growing: it becomes bigger every single day. Heaven also grows according to its inhabitant's dreams and creations. Every person in Heaven does the will of God, but with this being said, every person is an individual with his or her individual dreams, gifting and desires.

On earth, people see a need, and with a good idea and foresight, other people will back them with either labor or resources. Something new for earth will then be created which will hopefully tempt people to buy and use. In this way, Heaven is similar; people will get ideas, they have support, and they create something new that they and others in Heaven can enjoy.

On earth, we all have varying degrees of occupational satisfaction, even though not all are doing what they were created to do. Hopefully, half of them at least would be engaged in jobs or careers that God wanted them to have. Job selection in Heaven is quite different: people first find out what they were created to do and then they work in that field. There are bakers baking bread; chefs creating meals in restaurants, florists arranging flowers, and there are builders creating things, etc. In summary: everyone really enjoys their work in Heaven.

Of course, Heaven has no sickness, so there are no doctors practicing medicine. Also, there are no family lawyers solving marriage breakdowns or any other negative situations. Neither are there people involved in criminal activity of any kind.

There is no money in Heaven because everything is free: your house or mansion (linked to rewards established on earth) is freely built for you according to the type of house you would love to live in. You can freely eat at restaurants; you can select clothes made by Heaven's fashion designers; you can pick up a take-away and spend time at home watching Heaven's type of DVD over the course of your leisure hours.

In Heaven, everybody is totally fulfilled. You may have more than one job: you may be training to do other jobs in colleges, so that you can have variety in what you do. Perhaps on earth, you may have wanted to be a chef and cater for large functions as a corporate caterer, but never had the time, or perhaps you couldn't afford to live on the low wages of an apprenticeship. In Heaven, you can be that chef and cook for some of the heroes of your faith, and have someone like Moses come out to the kitchen and personally thank you for the meal that you created.

A wonderful attribute about Heaven is that there is no envy or jealousy among its inhabitants. So even though some people have more reward and live perhaps a better life, no one would ever be jealous of them. If you manage to live a life on earth that allows you to be much rewarded in Heaven, other people who live with less than you, will love and honor you. Everyone loves each other and builds each other up. Those living with more reward help those with less, so as to mature and grow them to where they are.

In contrast to life on earth, opportunities in Heaven are more plentiful and beneficial in promoting personal improvement. For example: there are many golf courses available and golfers never tire of the challenges that these courses provide. On earth, you may not have ever had enough time to play more than twice a week to improve your game. In Heaven, you will have far more time for recreation. Unlike earthly employment, you won't be stressed about earning enough to pay ongoing bills. Professional coaches are available to freely help you improve your game. In fact, there will be every sport or hobby imaginable for you to engage in and for you to excel in, at your own pace.

The most exciting thing is that everyone will have the opportunity to meet Jesus, one on one, and to also meet our Heavenly Father and sit with Him. Jesus is all around Heaven and it would not be Heaven without Him. He will spend much time with everyone. He still teaches and you will be able to sit on the lush green grass to hear Him teach you new things. He is the perfect King and we will all serve Him as He has eternal dominion over all of us.

There will be perfect music in Heaven where the saints and angels will gather to worship Jesus and the Father. Times in the presence and glory of God will be remarkable and will energize you so that you can carry on during your day and do your job well.

Some people will have the privilege of being a dancer and they will worship God in dance. Others will be musicians and will play music in the Throne Room from time to time. Certain people will have a job that sees them spend more time than others worshipping or helping in worship in the Throne Room. If you really love to worship God, you can be sure that you will never be denied spending enough time in worship.

Heaven is a place of dreams. If you have a dream, Heaven is the place where you will see your dreams come to life. Heaven is dynamic and moves and grows according to its population, creativity and dreams. There is no striving, there is no sweat, nor is there is any chasing after money to pay the bills. Everything is free and everything that you do will be totally enjoyable, exciting and fulfilling.

My Testimony: A little over a year ago, my Pastor's wife, Robyn, came up with an idea for me to serve free coffee, tea, and hot chocolate in our Community Center where many poor and marginalized people come and visit each week. I was given a small coffee station and they named the service "Chat with Matt." Each Thursday and Friday, I serve my customers with what they want and with some of them, I listen to their stories or whatever. On the days when I'm not there, these people can buy the same drinks from our kitchen for fifty cents. I really love the job. I enjoy serving needy people and chatting to those who need to talk to someone who is happy to hear them.

Some six months ago, Jesus told me that I would have a coffee shop in Heaven and serve coffee there. I was thrilled. A few months ago, I helped a friend of mine called Harry to see a vision of Heaven and He ended up seeing my personal coffee shop. He said not only was he in my coffee shop but he said it was called "Matthew's coffee." The people of Heaven are already being served in that coffee shop and many of the saints who regularly drink there see my life on earth and intercede for me.

Jesus also told me years ago that I would be a teacher in Heaven. When I visited my home in Heaven, I was shown a professional office with cameras and all sorts of things that would allow me to record teachings on video and to write books. I am not only going to produce films and write books but I am going to lecture to eager students.

Now on earth, I serve coffee, I write books and I make YouTube videos. Today, I am doing a portion of what I will be doing in Heaven. One day in the future, I will be preaching and teaching people things from a church pulpit. I must wait for those doors to open. In the meantime, I will be writing books and making videos and serving coffee.

What is eternity going to be like for you? I encourage you to read more about Heaven so you can gain an eternal perspective on your life on earth. You see, I am doing much of what I will be doing for eternity, and with God's help, so can you.

CHAPTER 4
WILL ALL GO TO HEAVEN?

I have quoted part of this Scripture earlier, but I need to use it again. *"This is the testimony; that God has given us eternal life, and this life is in His Son. He who has the Son has life; he who does not have the Son of God does not have life. These things I have written to you who believe in the name of the Son of God, that you may know that you have eternal life and that you may continue to believe in the name of the Son of God."* 1 John 5:11-13.

If you have already surrendered your life to Jesus Christ, then you have eternal life living in you right now, and you are Heaven bound. If you are still not certain about this, I suggest that you pray to Jesus by faith to forgive you for all the wrong things you have ever thought, said and done. Ask Him to come into your life as your Lord and Savior. Then thank Him for hearing and answering your prayer and for giving you eternal life.

It's extremely important that you tell a mature Christian what you have done and ask them to teach you the things of God. Believe that when you sincerely prayed to Jesus to come into your life, He placed His Holy Spirit in you as a *guarantee* that you now belong to Him. Jesus said emphatically that He is the only way to God in John 14:6. Believe and receive God's anointing by the Holy Spirit, not as a feeling, but as a steadfast guarantee that you have become a child of God.

The word "guarantee" is a business term for a pledge: a deposit or down-payment towards a final transaction. For example, many shops will accept a lay-by for goods which will be paid for in full, later on. Jesus gives us His Holy Spirit, as His pledge of our future joys in Heaven and to enable us to live holy lives. The indwelling

Holy Spirit gives us revelation of God's Word and helps us to remember the things we read in God's Word; He comforts us; He encourages us; He guides us as He teaches us the things of God. (See John 16:1-15)

Over time, with our cooperation, the indwelling Holy Spirit gradually transforms our lives to line up with the Word of God. Another important work of the Holy Spirit is to gently convict us whenever we sin, so as to lead us to repentance. In contrast, the devil places condemnation onto us whenever we sin, so as rob us of inner peace and self-worthiness. Satan does this because one of his names is the "accuser" of the brethren. (Revelation 12:10)

It is important for every believer to always remember that when God the Father lovingly looks down at us, He no longer sees what we used to be, but He sees His Holy Spirit in us and joyfully says: "That's 'My' precious child."

There is a growing belief that is spreading around the world called Universalism. Like most of the devil's deceptions, this is by no means a new belief system, but it has a new audience among the modern seeker of God. I don't know much about the details of this belief, as I try to stay away from error, but some of its followers believe that Satan, his demons and all the people of earth, will be saved and will all go to Heaven one day. I want to tell you emphatically; this is heresy, because we learn in Revelation 20:10 that Satan will be cast into the lake of fire and brimstone and will be tormented day and night, forever and ever.

Jesus said: "He who believes in the Son has everlasting life; and he who does not believe the Son shall not see life, but the wrath of God abides on him." John 3:36. It's not that Satan doesn't believe in God, he trembles in his belief. (James 2:19) Satan and his demons know their destiny, but they want to take as many people whom Christ died for, with them.

Most people in my country, Australia, believe that if a person is not a murderer or a paedophile, they will be accepted into

Heaven. (Perhaps this is true in your country as well.) The average Aussie non-believer thinks that if they are essentially a good person, who doesn't deliberately hurt others, that God, in His perfect goodness, will welcome them into His Heaven. But this view, although hopeful and positive, is contrary to Scripture.

John, the close disciple of Jesus, not only wrote a Gospel account, but also three short Epistles and the Book of Revelation; here he wrote some very thought- provoking words: *"Blessed are those who do His* (Jesus) *commandments that they may have the right to the tree of life, and may enter through the gates into the city. But outside are dogs and sorcerers and sexually immoral and murderers and idolaters, and whoever loves and practices a lie."* *Revelation 22:14-15*

Jesus had earlier said to His disciples: *"He who has My commandments and keeps them, it is he who loves Me. And he who loves Me will be loved by My Father, and I will love him and manifest Myself to him." John 14:21.* The assumption that Jesus was making was that if a person truly loved Him, they would also honor Him by wanting to do what He has called them to do. In direct contrast: there are people who wear the name 'Christian' but they are in fact, lovers of this world.

The verse above prompted one of His disciples to ask Jesus how He was going to manifest Himself to them and not to the world at large. Jesus went on to explain: *"If anyone loves Me, he will keep My word; and My Father will love him, and We will come to him and make Our home with him. He who does not love Me does not keep My words; and the word which you hear is not Mine but the Father's who sent Me." John 14: 23-24*

I want to comment on my earlier quote in Revelation 22:14-15. A person who genuinely loves Jesus will automatically follow His commandments and by doing so, they will manifest His light to the world. They will enter into the Holy City of God and live eternally in Heaven.

My Testimony: *It's exciting to know that Jesus not only promised to manifest Himself to His obedient followers, but both He and the Father will make their home with these people on earth. I have been fortunate to have Jesus and the Father come and visit me in my home in visions. Jesus has come a lot more than the Father, but nonetheless, both have come and visited me.*

These verses can mean the Holy Spirit will come and make His home within us, but wider meaning can mean that the whole trinity can come and visit us. I share that the Father has come to visit me a number of times, not to rock the boat or cause you to doubt me. It is up to you and your theology to accept or reject that it happened as I said. I share it simply to spark faith in the hungry faithful, for them to believe for their own visitation.

I didn't start out obeying Jesus so that He would appear to me. I started to obey Jesus because I came across a group called "The Jesus Christians" who believed that we should live our life as a Christian doing what Jesus taught. They taught that the church had moved away from doing what Jesus taught and had put their emphasis on grace alone.

I could not remember all of the commands of Jesus, but the one that quickly came to my mind was to "give to everybody that asks of you," (Matthew 5:42) Because I live in a big city, I am often approached by beggars, so I decided to give $2.00 to everybody who asked me for money even when I hardly had enough for my own needs. (I have since discovered that beggars do not expect to receive large amounts of money, just one or two dollars at a time or even fifty cents.) Soon after that, maybe a year or so, I started having visions of Jesus. Yes indeed, Jesus was really manifesting Himself to me.

Years went on and I became a lot more Christ-like and started to really enjoy a life of obedience. I began to hear Jesus and the Holy Spirit more clearly and I was able to walk in the Spirit. I have become so happy with my relationship with Jesus and I look forward to spending a great fun-time in eternity with as much reward as possible.

Ephesians 5:3 warns us that *"no fornicator, unclean person, nor covetous man, who is an idolater, has any inheritance in the kingdom of Christ and God."* My Bible notes tell me that "idolatry is an aggravated form of self-love motivated by human ego-drive." People whom the Bible calls "idolaters" in the world are described in the following two Bible passages:

> *"Do not love this world or the things it offers you, for when you love the world, you do not have the love of the Father in you. For the world offers only a craving for physical pleasure, a craving for everything we see, and pride in our achievements and possessions. These are not from the Father, but are from this world. And this world is fading away, along with everything that people crave. But anyone who does what pleases God will live forever."* 1 John 2:15-17 (New Living Translation)

> *"And even when you ask, you don't get it because your motives are all wrong - you want only what will give you pleasure. You adulterers! Don't you realize that friendship with the world makes you an enemy of God? I say it again: If you want to be a friend of the world, you make yourself an enemy of God."* James 4:3-4 (New Living Translation)

We learn from these passages that it's important not to be a friend of the world and its lusts. Here, the word "world" refers to the world system; to all its values, mind-sets, philosophies of life, and priorities that run contrary to the will and ways of God. James says that when you are a friend of the world, you become an enemy of God. And the question must be asked, how many enemies of God do you think He lets into His home? Whereas 1 John 2:17 promises that *"anyone who does what pleases God will live forever."*

Jesus gave His commandments so that we could not only live God-pleasing lives but that we could live a happier and more fulfilled life. After the resurrection, Paul wrote many of the New Testament Epistles which teach Christians how to successfully live life seated in Heavenly places. Both the teaching of Jesus and the teaching of Paul are relevant today.

Unlike the Old Testament believers, we have the grace of God freely given to us and also, we have the indwelling Holy Spirit's power, so obedience is no longer burdensome. However, it seems to me that many people have no idea that Jesus has even given us commandments, let alone expects us to live a life of obedience to them.

People only think about the Ten Commandment that God gave to the Israelites and are quick to say that Christians are no longer under the Law. The Ten Commandments are only a small part of the Law. The "Torah" or the Law makes up the first five books of the Bible that were written by Moses under the inspiration of the Holy Spirit. I believe there are 313 individual laws in the Torah so I am very relieved that we are not made right with God by law-keeping. Instead, we are made right with God by believing and personally knowing His Son.

I believe that God's overall desire in the Old Testament covenant was summarized in the following verse: *"He has shown you, O man, what is good; and what does the Lord require of you, but to do justly, to love mercy, and to walk humbly with your God." Micah 6:8.*

Whereas, I believe that God's overall desire in the New Testament was revealed to us when the disciples asked Jesus what was the "work" they were to do? He replied: *"This is the work of God that you believe in Him whom He sent." John 6:29.* Jesus was saying – it's not what you do, it's who you believe that's important, because right believing results in right doing.

Although equal with God in every way, Jesus, while on earth, willingly adopted a subservient role. He repeatedly said in the Gospel of John, that He only ever said and did what His Father told

Him to. Therefore, it seems logical to me, that we should obey the commands of Jesus. This seems to be especially true, because unlike the people in the Old Testament, we have the ongoing assistance of the indwelling Holy Spirit to empower us to be obedient to God.

Before Jesus could begin His earthly ministry, it was necessary for Him to be water baptized and filled with Holy-Spirit-power for service to others. At His baptism, an audible voice thundered from the Father in Heaven – introducing His Son: *"This is My beloved Son, in whom I am well pleased." Matthew 3:17.* Later, in this same Gospel account, we read that Jesus was gloriously transfigured in front of Peter, James and John. For the second time, the same thundering voice from Heaven declared: *"This is My beloved Son, in whom I am well pleased. Hear Him." Matthew 17:5.* We are to listen and pay attention to the words of Jesus!

You can do a search on Google with search string "The fifty commands of Jesus" and see what I discovered quite a few years ago. I'm certainly not trying to introduce a theology of legalism, as this is what the devil would delight in. I was bound in legalism nearly all my Christian life and I am so grateful that I no longer have to try to impress God to have Him love me. I know by experience that works done in the flesh simply don't cut it with God. He is not deceived for He sees our heart's motive.

After over thirty years of trying to earn God's favor, I finally received the revelation that set me free. *I already have God's favor* and His acceptance only came from believing in the work of Jesus. No works of mine can add to that! I first accepted Jesus as my personal Savior when I was only eight years old and spiritually, I was instantly translated into God's Heavenly Kingdom. The indwelling Holy Spirit is my on-going guarantee that I am fully accepted by God. The presence of the Holy Spirit in me causes me to "want" to please Him.

Revelation 22:14-15 which I quoted earlier, says that liars will be kept out of the Holy City. People may think this verse refers to someone who occasionally lies, but interestingly, John in the following verse gives us an idea of someone who is "practicing" a lie.

"Now by this we know that we know Him, if we keep His commandments. He who says, "I know Him," and does not keep His commandments, is a liar, and the truth is not in him." 1 John 2: 3-4. These words of John are hard words, but Jesus had earlier said a similar thing.

"Jesus said to the Jews who believed Him 'If you abide in My word, you are My disciples indeed and you shall know the truth, and the truth shall make you free.'" John 8:31-32.He later went on to say to these same people *"Most assuredly, I say to you, if anyone keeps My word he shall never taste death"* John 8:52b.

It should be coming clear about now that we need to know the commandments of Jesus and to start to obey them in the power of the Holy Spirit, in our day-to-day life. I say this because I have discovered that some Christians in the grace movement, even though they have great truths in their teaching, may be quite strong in their view that a Christian doesn't need to obey the commands of Jesus. They teach instead that Jesus did for us on the Cross all that we ever need to inherit salvation and as I have said earlier, I wholeheartedly agree. We can't add "our own works" to the finished work of Jesus on the cross.

The truth of the matter as I see it: if we truly love Jesus, the Holy Spirit in us will give us both the "desire" and the "ability" to obey His commands. This to my mind is confirmed by Paul: *"For it is God who works in you both to will and to do for His good pleasure." Philippians 2:13.*

This paraphrase resonates in my spirit. "It is God who gives me the desire and the ability to do His will. I am not to complain and argue, but I am to be a blameless and innocent child of God without fault in the midst of a lost generation. I am to shine as a bright star in a dark world and to hold fast the word of life until Christ comes for me." Philippians 2:14-16.

It is impossible for man to obey the commands of Jesus without the Holy Spirit, *but every Christian is never without the Holy Spirit - He lives in us: wherever we go, He goes.* That's why we should not go to places that would cause Him to feel uncomfortable. Nor should we expose our eyes to things that would grieve Him. Like the Psalmist, we should pray: *"Turn away my eyes from looking at worthless things, and revive me in Your ways" Psalm 119:37.*

We have the Bible's assurance that God truly loves His people and He's not going to desert us and leave us to look after ourselves. He promised Moses in *Deuteronomy 31:6*, He promised Joshua in *Joshua 1:5* and He has promised us in Hebrews 13:5b, *that He would not ever leave us or forsake us.*

Jesus has given every believer the power of the Holy Spirit to assist them to obey His commands. Yes, we are saved only by believing in the grace of God, through faith in His awesome goodness demonstrated on the Cross. Therefore, out of thankfulness for His love towards us, we should want to honor Him by obeying His commands as much as possible.

His commands teach us how to live with others in a caring and loving environment. His commands teach us how we can stand out as His light in our community, so as to draw others to Him. Although we may fail miserably many times, we need to know that our Heavenly Father wants us to be Christ-like in all our actions, thoughts and speech. We have God's anointed Handbook and His Holy Spirit to both teach and equip us to do His will.

Jesus continually glorified His Father. Now on earth, the Holy Spirit yearns to continually glorify Jesus through us. God wants us to live an abundant life and obeying the words of Jesus promotes that type of life. God also wants us to be His witnesses: His light and salt to the unsaved who are watching us. Obeying Jesus glorifies the Father and it personally gives us the best life. Our obedience will draw others to the Savior: people will want for themselves the peace and security that we possess. Instead of being deceived by the devil all the time, people need to see a better way to live.

All the verses I have quoted need to be reflected upon because all of them were inspired by the Holy Spirit. There is a mixture of both pre-cross and post-cross verses, but they all are part of the overall incorruptible Word of God which is relevant for all people for all time.

To come back to my chapter heading: Will all people go to Heaven? The answer is "No." Jesus Himself said in Matthew 7:13-14 that narrow is the path to eternal life and few find it and wide is the path that leads to destruction and many travel on it. Jesus becomes our Savior the moment we ask Him into our life, but having Him as Lord in our life in not an instantaneous reality. It is through the ongoing process of sanctification and the revelation knowledge of God's Word that we allow Him to be our actual Lord.

We are not to become legalistic about such matters. My grandmother came to the Lord at ninety-four years old. She had been involved in the occult for over fifty years and while still a baby Christian, she died. She came to know Jesus as Savior but not as Lord because of her failing health and the time factor, but I know that she is in Heaven. The same happened to the repentant thief on the cross and would have happened to many other people.

Many Christians around the world are not living a life of self denial, they are not living a life where they take up their personal cross each day, and they are not obeying the commands of Jesus in any practical way. I am definitely not implying that Christians are going to go to Hell. Not at all! I am not in favor of people who preach that sort of perverted theology.

What I am saying here is that if you want to live in the light of eternity, all the things I am discussing need to be looked at more seriously. Jesus Himself said narrow is the path that leads to life. Unbelievers, in their own strength, are certainly not willing to surrender their self-centredness which has controlled them from birth. It's only the Holy Spirit that empowers people to want to change. We are to work with the Holy Spirit for that change to be evidenced by others, so that God will be glorified to those not yet saved. I see obedience as an integral part of evangelism.

Jesus said to follow Him and He will make us fishers of men. Acting in humility, like Jesus did on earth, overrides self-centredness and this is what Jesus wants from His body – His church and His beautiful and radiant Bride (Male and female). For Jesus to be truly Lord of our life, our free-will in our soul area must learn to surrender to His will by the power of God Himself, that is, through the indwelling Holy Spirit in every Christian.

As I said before: it is God who works in you both to will and to do for His good pleasure. We can be very confident that Jesus will never call us to do anything for His glory, without first equipping us and giving us the desire to fulfil that call. This is a very exciting and comforting truth.

CHAPTER 5
LIFE TODAY – HOW DOES THAT COUNT?

We know that if we regularly save money in a bank and keep on putting some more away, that one day, we will have enough to buy something very special. On a far grander scale, many people know that if they genuinely accept Jesus Christ as their personal Lord and Savior, they will spend eternity living in God's home in Heaven.

Placing your life in the hands of Jesus is something far more than just repeating a brief prayer. This is because God, in His supernatural knowledge and grace, sees our heart. So very often, a brief prayer is all that we initially need to become His child. Out of ignorance, many of us give Jesus access to some parts of our life, but we automatically hold back other areas from Him. In other words, a new believer initially just wants Jesus to be their Savior but they do not realize that being their Savior gives Him the right to actually rule their life.

I liken this to a shopkeeper who has purchased a new business premise. When this new owner displays an "Under New Management" sign on the door, others in the area will know that things may be different than what they were before. In the same way, many Christians have invited Jesus into their life. In doing so, they have come under new management and in their heart, they know that a change has gloriously taken place.

Water baptism is a wonderful opportunity for new Christians to publicly let their friends and family know that a "change of management" has inwardly occurred in their life, which will cause them to be outwardly different to what they were before.

Initially, people respond to the Gospel because they want Jesus to save them from judgment and Hell. Many of these new converts do not fully understand the concept of Jesus being Lord of their life. That's one of the reasons why every new Christian should be taught by a mature believer, the basic Bible truths and their new Heavenly position in Christ. By just attending a weekly church service, a baby Christian's faith may takes years to develop because Satan will hinder them from discovering their new Kingdom birthrights.

I can honestly testify that "obeying the commands of Jesus" takes a believer into a deeper relationship with God. Some believers have been threatened with the possibility of losing their salvation and going to Hell if they don't obey God, but this kind of teaching only leads people into bondage. Satan just loves all forms of legalism because he loves to bind people up and to keep them bound.

Hell-fire preachers try to scare people into coming to Christ and many of those who respond to such a call eventually fall by the wayside. Hell certainly scares people, but an unhealthy "fear of God" doesn't enable a person to become holy and righteous. Rather, it is the very opposite! It is the knowledge of the "goodness of God" that will cause a person to want to live a holy life. When we know His absolute goodness, we will also have a positive and healthy reverent fear of God, because He is so holy.

Paul had better things to talk about than the religious leaders of his day. Paul led by example. He knew the importance of controlling his thought life as our thoughts lead us to produce either positive or negative actions. Contrary to modern day thinking, not all knowledge is good. Our prayer should be "Have Your way in me, Lord."

God wants us to be wise but not in ALL things. He wants us to be *"wise in what is good, and simple concerning evil." Romans 16:19b.* God wants us to be ignorant and innocent like a young child concerning evil. He wants us to be pure and urges us to have positive thoughts.

Thoughts are important because they produce actions. Paul said: *"Finally, brethren, whatever things are true, whatever things are noble, whatever things are just, whatever things are pure, whatever things are lovely, whatever things are of good report, if there is any virtue and if there is anything praiseworthy - meditate on these things." Philippians 4:8*

We are to talk about the good and honorable things, and encourage people in their faith, rather than beat them down with destructive negativity. Let me share a story with you.

My Testimony: Here is a good story to think about. For many years, I lived with one foot in the Old Testament and one foot in New Testament grace. I lived a mixed-up life and didn't fully believe that God's grace saved me. I had read books on Hell and lived in fear of going there because of my sinful lifestyle. I even preached on YouTube, wrote articles, and ran a prophetic website to sort of buy "Eternity Insurance" in case Jesus' blood was not enough to cleanse me of my sin. I was always preaching on what believers should do to live a holy life and how far short the average Christian was in their walk with God, even though I wasn't seeing any success in personal holiness.

At the time, I knew a lovely girl who was my friend. She was so patient and kind to me. Looking back now, she was really long-suffering for I was always pointing my finger at everyone but myself. One day, she lovingly gave me a portion of a book called "The Prodigal God" and told me to read a particular passage. The part highlighted for me to read was a portion that spoke about the prodigal son's older brother and how he was full of pride and self-righteousness and how that attitude was so distressing to his father. In my mind, the passage clearly identified me as being this older brother! I was stunned and soon, my friend saw an opening in my beliefs and followed it up with another book that was all about God's incredible grace.

This grace revelation eventually changed my view of God. I was turned right around by God's awesomeness displayed in the finished work of the cross. However, it took me years to conquer my addictive sin. This happened when I had finally seen that I was loved by God no matter if I had sinned or not. It was only when I saw myself as being loved whilst "in my sin" and only when I came to the end of myself and asked God for the power to conquer my sin, that I was set free. For years, I had suffered under that sin and under tremendous guilt and condemnation. So I am the first to admit that scaring people doesn't work - in fact, fear keeps people in bondage. It is only the revelation of the "goodness" of God that leads to lasting repentance.

When I discovered God's grace, I felt that I was born again anew. My life was transformed.

Jesus said: *"Come to Me, all you who labor and are heavy laden, and I will give you rest. Take My yoke upon you and learn from Me, for I am gentle and lowly in heart, and you will find rest for your souls. For My yoke is easy and My burden is light."* Matthew 11:28-30

According to my Bible notes, "the word 'easy' denotes that which is useful, pleasant, good, comfortable, suitable and serviceable. In the days of Jesus, the legalistic religious system was a severe burden, but service to Jesus does not chafe, because it is well-fitting and built on personal relationship with God by the indwelling Spirit."

Paul said *"Stand fast therefore in the liberty by which Christ has made us free, and do not be entangled again with a yoke of bondage."* Galatians 5:1. Put on the easy yoke of Jesus.

Though we are saved by the cross of Jesus alone, the Christian life can be a better and richer life when we "walk in obedience" to God. Jesus has many good things in mind for people who are obedient to Him and are open to His desires for them. Obedience proves to God that you truly want to honor Him out of a heart full of gratitude to Him.

Your earnest desire to press into God will thrust you into a more fulfilling life here on earth and it will better prepare you for a life in eternity. Discovering that you are a wonderful creation and finding what you are here for and taking the steps to walk in that calling will bring you much satisfaction. As you walk hand in hand with Jesus, it is possible to do many good works that will bring glory to God.

Paul said: *"For we are His workmanship, created in Christ Jesus for good works, which God prepared beforehand that we should walk in them."* Ephesians 2:10

I once heard in a sermon that the term "His workmanship" means in the Greek: "exquisite masterpiece." Have you ever thought of yourself like that? Many of us have such a low opinion of ourselves that we can't easily grasp that to God, we are an exquisite masterpiece. In fact, we all need personal revelation from God, or tremendous encouragement by others, or by God's prophets, to accept and believe that we are indeed God's precious masterpiece.

In the last nine months, I have been part of a Facebook Group called *"Inside Out Training and Equipping School."* This is a school of the supernatural on Facebook where Christians meet and have training through Skype. In the past nine months, I have had about fifty prophecies over my life and in every one of these prophetic words, I have heard what God thinks of me and what my potential is. I have grown much in these last nine months and have come to love myself a whole lot better. Now I really know that I am valuable and precious to God and that one day, I am going to be a force to be reckoned with for God's Kingdom purposes.

Ask God to help you see yourself as His exquisite masterpiece. God has a special purpose for you. If you don't know what you are called to do, it would be helpful for you to mix with prophetic people who can see your gifts and talents and encourage you to walk in them.

Jesus has saved you and He has led you to this book. The fact that you are reading it now means that you want your life to count in eternity. The fact that you are in the fifth chapter means that you are keen to learn. That's good news! Here are some more good news. The Apostle Paul said: *"being confident of this very thing, that He who has begun a good work in you will complete it until the day of Jesus Christ." Philippians 1:6.*

Paul again encourages us that Jesus Christ *"will also confirm you to the end, that you may be blameless in the day of our Lord Jesus Christ. God is faithful, by whom you were called into the fellowship of His Son, Jesus Christ our Lord."* 1 Corinthians 1:8-9

Paul, who had suffered terribly for his faith in God, wrote in his letter to young Timothy: *"The Lord will deliver me from every evil work and preserve me for His Heavenly kingdom. To Him be glory forever and ever. Amen!" 2 Timothy 4:18.*

Just in case you still worry about the fruit of your salvation, Paul assures us all with his mighty prayer: *"Now may the God of peace Himself sanctify you completely, and may your whole spirit, soul, and body be preserved blameless at the coming of our Lord Jesus Christ. He who calls you is faithful who also will do it."* 1 *Thessalonians 5: 23-24*

Can God do anything He puts His mind to? Of course! Then know that He is going to perfect us, we just need to let Him do it by working with Him and not against Him.

If you are born again, I know that you want your life to really count. In fact, you are so interested that you have read past a hard chapter about denying yourself and taking up your cross! You then went on to read about how important it is to obey Christ Jesus. You persisted to read because you are keen to make your life count. The fact that you are still reading means you are teachable and more humble than most people. I believe that the Holy Spirit designed the book with those tough hurdles for you to jump over.

God has begun a great work in you and He will complete the work that He started in you right until the time that Jesus comes to take you to Himself. Yes, your life counts. Yes, there is much in life that you can do that will have eternal value. Yes, you have made a good start. Now, let me pray for you.

Dear Father, So far, there has been much that could have offended this reader. Denying oneself and taking up a cross is not popular these days. Hearing that you have visited me on earth multiple times did not put this reader off. Being told that they need to obey the commands of Jesus did not stop them reading. I can only conclude that this reader is very hungry for You and wants with all their heart for their life to count in the scheme of eternity.

Father, I pray that you anoint the reader now with your Spirit and that you give them the desire to keep reading to the end of this book. I pray that you teach them and encourage them to pull out all Your truths, until they receive revelation from Yourself directly into their own heart. I pray that they will read this book to the end and even return to it time and time again until this message becomes part of their life and witness.

Lord, touch the reader, teach them and impart Your grace to them so that they, too, can live a life of destiny like I am so blessed to live through You. In Jesus' name, I ask, Amen.

CHAPTER 6
FINDING PURPOSE TODAY

Bill Vincent, in his book, *"Glory: Increasing God's Presence"* says: *"Your destiny, my destiny, the relationship, the anointing, the soul, the harvest, the gifts, the talents – it is worth the fight, it is worth rescue, it is worth restoration, it is worth repentance, it is worth forgiveness, it is worth cultivating, it is worth lingering with God and moving on and moving with God into the manifestation of His promises, for His Own sake.*

2 Timothy 1:12 – For which cause I also suffer these things; nevertheless I am not ashamed; for I know whom I have believed, and I am persuaded that He is able to keep that which I have committed unto Him against this day."

God wants to release His Kingdom on earth through us, in the power of His Holy Spirit. The Spirit's work in us is to gradually transform us into the image of Jesus Christ so that we can reflect His nature in the world. We don't need to be a pastor, teacher, apostle, prophet or evangelist to fulfil God's purposes as God just wants us to surrender ourselves to Him so that we can be an influence for good in our unique area of influence.

"Whoever keeps His word, truly the love of God is perfected in him. By this we know that we are in Him. He who says he abides in Him ought himself also to walk just as He walked." 1 John 2:5-6. I'm not sure if I have ever heard anyone preach on the last part of this quote.

Many people know about Jesus and they regularly attend church, but much fewer of them can claim that they "abide" in Jesus. The public evidence of someone abiding in Christ will be openly displayed by their speech and behavior. Inward confirmation that we are truly abiding in Christ is evidenced by the fact that we constantly keep His word in mind. We are not only to believe His Word, but we are to live our lives following the example of Jesus.

We need spiritual stability to discover our life purpose. When we see ourselves as God sees us, Satan will not be able to derail us from finding our purpose in life. Yes, in the flesh, we are weak, but in Christ, we are strong, in fact, we are more than conquerors through Him who loved us. (Romans 8:37) We are to see ourselves seated in Heavenly places with God.

Christians have a much higher privilege than the heirs of the British Monarchy! I want to assure my reader that if they are "in Christ," then they are not to let their body, or their soul, or the devil, sow seeds of doubt about the entitlements of their Heavenly position. In regard to this, I will quote some of what Dr Ken Chant teaches in Vision International College manual called "Throne Rights" in his Lesson One. I will use italics for this direct quote.

"The throne He has given me is no mere ceremonial piece; it is replete with power, its sceptre is mighty, it dominion as wide as God's own, its crown fully of glory. This is a sovereignty like that represented in Scripture, where the king speaks and the whole earth hastens to do his bidding.

But all who claim royal lineage must be able to produce a patent of their high birth; that is, documentary evidence to establish their right to the throne. Can I do this? Yes, I can. And so can you. For God has granted you the same elevation as He has for me - this enthronement comes to us through Christ, and we have the strongest possible claim to it: it is ours by right of birth, by right of adoption, and by right of conquest.

There are those who are kings because they are born with a crown upon their heads; there are those who are kings because they have been adopted into a royal family; and there are those who have seized a throne by force. But in all history, only God's

48

chosen people hold the throne by this triple right! Their claim could hardly be more secure. No coup against them can hope to succeed. No insurrection can disturb their dominion. Their sovereignty is invincible!

Your right to the throne is established by the new birth, which has made you the Father's child; by adoption in Christ, which had doubly strengthened your legal claim and by conquest, through your access by faith to the triumph of Christ's resurrection and ascension."

Believers have triple right to God's Throne. If you have become united with Christ through faith, then it is true to say that when Christ rose from the dead, you rose with Him; when Christ ascended into Heaven, you ascended with Him; when Christ sat down at the right hand of the Majesty on High, you sat down with Him.

The Risen Lord Jesus is enthroned *"far above all principality and power and might and dominion, and every name that is named, not only in this age but also in that which is to come. And He put all things under His feet and gave Him to be head over all things to the church, which is His body, the fullness of Him who fills all in all."* Ephesians 1:21-23

Can you see why I say that all those in Christ have a brand new identity and this is how Father God continually views us? We are to do likewise, for when we change our old carnal mindset to line up with our new position in Christ, we will no longer be tossed around by our own wrong thinking or by the devil. Over time, we will be guided into our purpose because we will want God to have His perfect way in our life.

Jesus, in His short life on earth, consistently overcame the temptations and power of Satan. His final victory was His bodily resurrection He not only defeated physical death but totally stripped Satan of his power. (Colossians 1:15) This victory over Satan that Jesus won "for us" is the spiritual birthright of every

Christian at the moment of their salvation prayer.

God the Father knows our heart and His will for us. Not only that, we have the best intercessor ever, praying for us - *"Likewise the Spirit also helps in our weaknesses. For we do not know what we should pray for as we ought, but the Spirit Himself makes intercession for us with groaning which cannot be uttered." Romans 8:26*

One of the most God-glorifying things any Christian can do is to live their life in such a way that people observe their words and actions and simply say to themselves - "Praise God!" To bring God glory could be – "to make God praise-worthy in someone else's opinion." That would be a truly great achievement. Our purpose in life is to be the best that we can be, with the Holy Spirit's enabling power. God doesn't want us to struggle through life, as things done in the flesh only bring praise from man, not from God.

Instead, God wants us always to avail ourselves to His enabling grace and power, so as to overcome and achieve great things for Him on earth. We are to never underestimate the power of God in our life for it is more powerful than our wildest dreams. *"Now to Him who is able to do exceedingly abundantly above all that we ask or think, according to the power that works in us." Ephesians 3:20.* God has big dreams for His family!

I will now share a little of my testimony: *When I was seventeen years old, my English teacher gave me back my homework. He had marked it ten out of ten! I had never had English homework returned to me with no red correction marks as I was hopeless with spelling and grammar. The highest mark I had ever had up till then had been eight out of ten. I looked at the teacher with a question on my lips and he told me to meet with him after class.*

Later, my teacher took me aside and said: "Matthew, the reason I didn't correct any of your spelling and grammar was because I wanted you to remember this day. As an English teacher, it is my job to teach students how to write good compositions and how to have accurate spelling and grammar. When a student has as many mistakes as you do in their grammar and spelling, the maximum mark I can give them for their work is eight out of ten. In my class, you have received quite a lot of eights haven't you?"

I nodded.

"Matthew, I don't believe that you are ever going to have good spelling and grammar! It simply isn't in you. But you are one of the best young writers I have ever seen. I want you to remember that and make sure you keep writing. There are heaps of people with good English skills who can make your grammar and spelling perfect, but there are few writers of your skill. Promise me that you will consider writing more when you leave school."

I promised him.

Now this book is the seventh book that I have written. I cannot do anything but praise God for that teacher and that perfect mark he gave me that day. Who would think that a person who failed English in high school would go on to write seven books? I believe that God took the words of my English teacher and planted them like a seed in my heart so that I would one day have the burning desire and the necessary boldness to write about the goodness of God."

I will now share some teaching from Pastor Andrew Wommack from Colorado Springs, USA. In his study manual called *"Discipling Through Romans,"* he expounds Romans 8:29 *"Whom He **foreknew**, He also **predestined** to be conformed to the image of His Son, that He might be **the firstborn** among many brethren."Romans 8:29* (Emphasis is mine)

Foreknew: Believers were chosen in Christ before the foundation of the world (Ephesians 1:4) God knows our choices in advance yet there are some things God Himself said He had never foreseen – see Jeremiah 19:5 and 32:35. He stopped Abraham from sacrificing his son and said *"now I know that you fear God, since* *you have not withheld your son, your only son from Me." Genesis 22:12.* Also, God repented that He had chosen Saul to be king, when he saw the way he turned out – see 1 Samuel 15:11

It is most probable that the Lord has the ability to know everything in advance, but He simply doesn't choose to exercise that ability in every situation. He told us to be wise concerning that which is good and simple (or innocent) concerning that which is evil – Romans 16:19. He also told us to think on praise worthy things in Philippians 4:8 – that's the way He wants us to be because that's the way He is.

Predestined: Predestination is dependent on foreknowledge. God already knew who would accept His offer of salvation long before the foundation of the earth: *"Just as He chose us in Him before the foundation of the world, that we should be holy and without blame before Him in love, having predestined us to adoption as sons by Jesus Christ to Himself, according to the good pleasure of His will." Ephesians 1:4-5.*

That's how infinite God's ability is to know our choices in advance. This verse assures us that becoming a Christian was our "destiny" in life. God not only saw that we were to be saved from the penalty of sin, but He went beyond that; He has brought us into His Own Royal Family and has made us co-heirs with Christ.

John says in His Epistle: *"Love has been perfected among us in this; that we may have boldness in the Day of Judgment; because as He is, so are we in this world." I John 4:17.* Think about it – *"as He is, so are we in this world."* God wants our self-image to line up with His Word. Note: John 4:17 has three different tenses: the first part is past-tense, the second part is future tense and the last part is present tense. In God's sight, right now, we are already like Jesus because every believer's spirit has God in it.

The firstborn - Jesus *"was to be the 'firstborn' among many brethren."* Andrew Wommack explains that what Christ modelled on earth is to be our life time goal. Salvation is the starting point,

from the very start to the very end. He that begun a good work in us at salvation and sees us as "perfect" right through until the very end of our days on earth. Yes, "perfect" because God is looking at our spirit, the real us, and His Holy Spirit has already perfected our human spirit.

"What then shall we say to these things? If God is for us, who can be against us? He who did not spare His own Son, but delivered Him up for us all, how shall He not with Him also freely give us all things?" Romans 8:31-32. If God did not spare His own Son, but gave Him as a sacrifice for us, won't He then freely give us everything that we need in order for us to achieve His will on earth? This passage is an exclamation of victory for the Spirit controlled life. Paul continues through in victory and praise to the end of Romans Chapter 8.

God has chosen us before the earth was created, He knew that we would respond to Him. Jesus continues to pray God's will in our life, so it doesn't really matter what we have previously been up to, because God now resides in us. In all things, we can be confident that God will work together for our good. (Romans 8:28) We are to go on and pursue God and his purposes for us. If we have been predestined, chosen, called, and justified by God, then what or who, can stand against us from doing God's will in our life when Jesus is praying in Heaven for us?

Perhaps, you have never seen this passage of Scripture in this light. I have to join you. I am so glad that God uses anointed teachers who are gifted to pull verses apart. I am personally indebted to Andrew Wommack as he was used by the Holy Spirit to teach truth in such a way that my life was radically transformed. God's on our side and wants us to glorify Him.

Once we are saved, God always sees us as being crucified with Christ. Because God has perfected our spirit, we need to focus on re-programming our "mind" so that our thoughts become lined up to what God says. Unfortunately, unlike a computer, our mind doesn't have a delete key, so we continually need the help of the Holy Spirit to re-program our thought life. The only way we can delete wrong programming built up since birth is by continually soaking our mind in the Word of God. It's liberating to learn that we don't have to be a slave to sin anymore, but through the renewing of our minds, we can actually *do the will of God.*

When we truly see our carnal self as being crucified with Christ and our new spiritual self being as perfect as God, then we will be walking in the liberty that Christ died for. Our thought life is so important. Paul said it this way: *"For those who live according to the flesh set their minds on the things of the flesh, but those who live according to the Spirit, the things of the Spirit. For to be carnally minded is death, but to be spiritually minded is life and peace." Romans 8:5-6*

These verses describe two opposing laws: the law of sin and the law of the Spirit. The law of sin will bring some form of death into a situation, whereas the Spirit will bring life into the same situation. Here God teaches us to choose life so that the outcome will be good. We are not to dwell on bad situations or outcomes – this type of negative thinking is called "carnal" thinking – *it feeds the law of sin.* Instead, when bad things happen, we are to choose to be spiritual minded and thank God that He will work in the situation to bring a God glorifying outcome. So often, we do the very opposite and just dwell on the negative aspect.

For example: If a loved one is seriously injured and you just dwell on what you see, or what you have been told by the doctor, you will encourage "death" into the situation. But if you reach out in faith to God and dwell on a positive outcome, you will bring life and peace into the situation. It is so important to be absolutely convinced that God is good always.

Romans 8:5-6 quoted above is a "law" of God, every bit as powerful as the law of gravity. God's laws can counter one another. For example, a heavy plane can fly simply because of

God's law of aerodynamics; this law cancels the law of gravity. But if for some reason the engines stops, the law of gravity would cause the plane to crash. Both natural and spiritual Laws of God always work because God made them to always work.

Jesus said: *"It is the Spirit who gives life; the flesh profits nothing. The words that I speak to you are spirit, and they are life." John 6:63.* Therefore, the way to be spiritually minded is to be "Word-of- God" minded, especially concerning the "grace" of God. When you are relating to God based on His grace – what He has done for you in your faith response to Him – then, you have life and peace. Anything contrary to this could be fleshly or carnal mindedness.

Being carnal is not necessarily a terrible sin or being rebellious. Being carnal-minded is just being religious, legalistic, or trying to relate to God by Old Covenant Law. Carnal or fleshly thoughts can never produce life and peace, but can actually cause bad outcomes.

In whatever purpose God has for you today, most of all, He wants you to glorify His name by being Christ-like towards others. Maybe you have never seen your purpose in this way. As a writer who serves coffee and one day will be invited to preach in pulpits, my chief purpose is not to write, nor to serve coffee, nor to preach, but my life's chief purpose is to bring glory to the Name of God and for people to look at my life and say, "Praise God!"

This chapter will be probably the longest and most theological one in this book as I drew on the teaching of others. However, I trust that it has blessed my reader.

CHAPTER 7
LIVING WITH EYES FIXED ON REWARD

Jesus had much to say about life on earth, but some of us read the Bible and just gloss over much of it. For instance, if a particular Scripture is about salvation, we may assume it doesn't apply to us because we are already saved. The point I want to make is that God's Word speaks to us where we are at, it is a "living" word. It goes on talking to us all the time as we progress at different levels. For example: let's read two parables found in Matthew 13:44-46.

> 1.   The first parable in Matthew 13:44 says: *"Again, the kingdom of Heaven is like treasure hidden in a field, which a man found and hid; and for joy over it he goes and sells all that he has and buys that field."*

This verse is talking about salvation which is offered only by Jesus. Preachers rightly teach that Jesus is the hidden treasure in the field and we are the person that sells all we own to buy the field and possess the treasure. But when did you or I ever purchase our relationship with Jesus? Would you be happy to give away everything, so that you could live a supernatural life for eternity?

Keeping Matthew 13:44 in mind, let's see what Jesus told the rich young ruler who wanted to inherit eternal life. This young man had boasted that he had kept all the commandments since a youth. Jesus wisely replied: *"You still lack one thing. Sell all that you have and distribute to the poor, and you will have treasure in Heaven, and come follow me." Luke 18:22.*

What is Jesus saying today to us, in these two stories? Would you be willing to exchange riches in this life, in order to receive all that Heaven has for you?

> 2. The second parable in Matthew 13:45-46 *"Again, the kingdom of Heaven is like a merchant seeking beautiful pearls, who when he had found one pearl of great price, went and sold all that he had and bought it."*

I have heard two different thoughts on this parable. One is that God was so sold out for us, that He allowed the horrific sacrifice of His one and only precious Son to purchase us. The alternate interpretation is: would we take all that we have achieved in life and give it up for Jesus, so that His good and perfect will can be demonstrated in our life? Are we really that sold out for God?

Most Christians I know won't even give two dollars to a homeless beggar on the street. I only know of two Christians who do this. Other friends of mine may privately do it, but since I started giving to beggars, I have only met two people like myself and one of them is my friend. Not only do Christians fail in this area, but few of them actually give anything substantial to the Lord in offerings and tithes.

Some believers today are adamant that the tithe is an Old Testament law and in the New Covenant of grace, Christians do not have to tithe. I disagree with this because I don't see giving tithes as being a money issue, but rather being a heart and faith issue. Probably I feel like I do because I have the confident assurance that God is a good God – always. My parents and two of my siblings also have proved time and time again, that no one can ever out-give God. He will simply not allow us to bless Him more than what He blesses us with.

As a sermon topic in a conservative church, teaching about giving is a big "No-no," and in many of the Pentecostal churches, the reverse is true. Although I love both kinds of worship, I really believe that some Pentecostals can, at times, go overboard in their claims. I liken some of what they preach to a financial adviser who has a vested interest in a product and stretches the returns, so that their clients invest more. With some people in the congregation, this sort of teaching can actually feed the carnal nature of man.

Then, there are also some Pentecostal pastors who are quite conservative in their approach to giving. Their focus is to teach their congregation about the love of Almighty God who said: *"I will not forget you. See, I have inscribed you on the palms of My hands."* Isaiah 49:16.

This approach I feel is better because when we have the confident assurance that our future is sure, we will want to give our tithes and offerings to God out of a thankful heart alone. We will know that in doing so, we are pleasing the God who is so very mindful of us.

Whether the subject of tithing is ignored, or if it's pushed to the extreme, people do have strong feelings on the subject of money. The answer on giving to God would be for all of us to receive a personal revelation from God. Both tithing and accumulating earthly treasures are matters of the heart. In Chapter Seventeen, I speak more on this important subject.

Jesus said: *"Do not lay up for yourselves treasures on earth, where moth and rust destroy and where thieves break in and steal; but lay up for yourselves treasures in Heaven, where neither moth nor rust destroys and where thieves do not break in and steal. For where your treasure is, there your heart will be also."* Matthew 6:19-21

That is so true. Would you be like that merchant who saw the pearl of great price and sold all that he had to possess it? When Jesus told us not to store up personal treasures on earth, He was inferring that our possessions on earth are not of any eternal consequence. No matter how big our house, no matter how many cars we have, and no matter how much money we have in the bank; when we die, we simply leave this earth with no earthly treasures at all.

The only personal contribution to your future life in Heaven is the treasure that you have already stored up there, by the Christ-like influence that you have left on others whilst on earth. I have spoken about this subject already in an earlier chapter. But how do you store treasures in Heaven? How do we become so committed to Jesus to a point where we will deny our lusts for the things of the world, in order to gain Heavenly treasures?

One thing I do know is that when you begin to store up treasures in Heaven, you will become Heavenly minded. I believe that the reason why I have so many supernatural encounters with Jesus, angels and the saints of God, is that my whole life is Heaven focused. I believe that treasures in Heaven are the things you do on earth that help people come to know about the love of Jesus. Acts of kindness will automatically convert to Heavenly treasure. I believe that these treasures can come from simple things such as:

- A friendly wave or a smile to a shop keeper each morning; being courteous to a server in a restaurant. Showing people the light of Christ in you always earns you treasure.

- When you give finances to mission organizations, you help widows to survive; you help orphans to be raised; you help people be saved through evangelistic outreaches – there are so many ways to store up treasures. There are many great organizations if you study and look for them, but if you really want to know some of the best ones I know, write to me and ask me at survivors.sanctuary@gmail.com.

- Anything you do to help a person grow in their relationship with Jesus who is already a Christian will gain you treasure. This can be giving a single mother a set-value credit card at a particular store, or buying a few bags of groceries. When you read any book that really helps you, even lending that book to a friend will earn you treasure. God loves his people growing in the knowledge of Him.

• Earning treasures do not even have to cost you financially. If you see a God glorifying YouTube video, you can post it on your friends' Facebook wall and tell them that it is really good and worth a watch.

• We can earn treasures by praying for people, teaching new Christians, giving to people, loving people and being Christ to those you meet. If someone has a gambling or drinking husband, you can take the wife and children shopping and earn treasures.

When you have spare money and a heart to share it, God will show you many ways to do so. Even when you see a "free" book on Facebook advertised, and it looks like a good one, sharing that with your friends will earn you treasures. The less we spend on our lavish lifestyles, the more we will have to bless people.

I saw a movie many years ago that was called: Pay It Forward. It was about a young lad who decided that whenever he received a personal act of kindness from someone, he would "pay forward the kindness" by doing a similar kind act to others. He ended up converting most of his town folk to do likewise. It was a feel-good movie and it definitely challenged me about the Gospel story. Every Christian has understood the extravagant kindness of God and we should, as we are able, to "pay forward" that kindness on to others.

My testimony: God is going to really surprise us beyond what we can conceive or believe is possible, with what he has stored up for us who are faithful to Him. As I have mentioned, I have gone to Heaven several times in visions and in dreams.

The first time I went to Heaven, I saw my home already built. It has a luxurious and functional kitchen with a center wash-up area, much like my much loved auntie and uncle's home as well as a swimming pool like they used to have. Outside, there is a huge expanse of water with sail boats sailing on it. I have a private pier and a cruiser that sleeps eight people. My auntie and uncle have lived in two homes with magnificent water views and Jesus would know that I would be surprised and thrilled.

I share these things so that you will know that Jesus will have a home ready for you that will be uniquely designed with you in mind. He already knows your taste in such matters but He delights to excel in fulfilling every dream.

The second time I went to Heaven, I saw that my home was three stories high. The inside had beautiful exposed beams and it had polished wooden floors throughout with colorful throw rugs. (The three homes I grew up in had polished floors but they were not as shiny as my home in Heaven.) A huge fireplace is in the living room and circular stairs lead up to the second level. Running down the inside walls are inbuilt fish tanks with colorful tropical fish gracefully swimming around. This might sound very strange, but the fish can actually swim into whatever room I walk into as if they want to follow me everywhere I go.

My dad is rather an eccentric fisherman and he would love my home in Heaven. When I was young, I envied the fact that my older cousin had a tropical fish tank for I loved to watch them when I visited him. Jesus knew my heart back then and put in this feature especially to surprise me. There is a very large painting of a lion and a lamb lying down peacefully together in the living room. These animals came to life when I looked at them, but they seemed to really love me. This particular painting acted somehow as a portal to another place in Heaven where children live.

On my third trip to Heaven, I met my cat that had died when I was eight years old. His death broke my heart at the time for I used to share all my deep things with him and I am sure he listened to my sad stories. In Heaven, my cat actually spoke to me. He even prophesied over me - He told me that my room-mate was going to move out from living with me with no fuss. I had been worried about telling him he had to go, but my cat assured me that it would work out fine.(This came true when my room-mate left and has remained a friend of mine.)

I want to assure my reader that if you are worried about your departed pet, then rest assured if you love Jesus, know that you will see this pet again, because my cat is well and happy. I believe that people who say pets don't go to Heaven are deceived by Satan. My cat recognized me even as an adult.

On one of my Heavenly visits, I also talked to a fish called Harry. This little creature spoke to me and reassured me that my whole future was planned and it was a good future, so I was to just take one day at a time. He told me that the Holy Spirit would continue to direct me and for me not to worry about anything, because I would know what to do and when to do it. Surprisingly, not long after this, I met a new friend whose name was also Harry. We both go out together sometimes and do prophetic evangelism on the streets.

I certainly don't consider myself a great person, but obviously, the Lord has seen fit to bless me abundantly – more than I could ever dream. Perhaps, He has rewarded me for the thousands of dollars I have already spent on His kingdom and the many years of service I will put in before I die or am taken by Jesus in the clouds. I have seen my house in Heaven and it certainly took my breath away. It went beyond my wildest imagination.

Once again, people might doubt a simple person like me could have already visited Heaven. They might not theologically be able to believe this, but I testify to God's faithfulness for the spiritually hungry believers so as to spark faith and hope in them to live a better life of service and self denial on earth. So far, I have visited *my home in Heaven on seven occasions. Honestly, just thinking about my wonderful rewards - makes me tear up as I type. Yes, I am very mindful of what I am headed for.*

What are you headed for? I guess going to Heaven and seeing your rewards there before you die is a little more of what Jesus might have meant when He said in Matthew 6:21 "For where your treasure is, there your heart will be also".

_____

CHAPTER 8
BEING FULFILLED TODAY

Andrew Wommack has preached an extensive series of sermons on finding your purpose on earth, and living in your destiny. On his ministry website, you can see him preaching to congregations where he invites the people who truly want to live in their purpose, to come forward for prayer. At least eighty percent of the believers come to the front to be prayed for. When I saw that, I was amazed that there were so many Christians who felt that they were not living in God's destined purpose for them.

Some believers may feel that they are living their Christian life like a fish in a fishbowl: they just aimlessly go round in circles. Some of them may know mentally that they are fully equipped to minister to others, but emotionally, they feel ill-equipped and this prevents them from doing God's will. When we doubt our ability concerning ministry, we unconsciously doubt the power of God living within us. The devil is a liar and a master at promoting doubt, especially when it comes to the things of God.

Jesus angrily said to the legalistic unbelieving Pharisees: *"You are of your father the devil, and the desires of your father you want to do. He was a murderer from the beginning, and does not stand in the truth, because there is no truth in him. When he speaks a lie, he speaks from his own resources, for he is a liar and the father of it."* John 8:44.

We are told to first, *"submit to God. Resist the devil and he will flee from you."* James 4:7 Submission to God empowers us to resist the devil and it causes him to flee. Also, be mindful of the awesome authority you have: *"He* (the Holy Spirit) *who is in us, is greater than he* (Satan) *who is in the world."* 1 John 4:4.

Feeling weak or inadequate can have one positive aspect, because we are told that -*"He* (God) *gives power to the weak, and to those who have no might He increases strength." Isaiah 40:29.* Jesus also wants us to rest in His strength. He said: *"My grace is sufficient for you, for My strength is made perfect in weakness."* Therefore, our response is to continually acknowledge that - *"When I am weak, then I am strong."* (See 2 Corinthians 12:9a and 10b)

We are to take comfort that in 1 Corinthians 1:25, we are told that: *"The foolishness of God is wiser than men, and the weakness of God is stronger than men."* Why? Because: *"God has chosen the foolish things of the world to put to shame the wise, and God has chosen the weak things of the world to put to shame the things which are mighty." 1 Corinthians 1:25, 27.*

In our own human strength, we are weak, but really, we are never alone. We have God's promise: *"I will never leave you nor forsake you. So we may boldly say: The Lord is my helper; I will not fear. What can man do to me?" Hebrews 13:5b-6*

As believers, we were not predestined, saved, called and justified, so that we can live a life without meaning or purpose. We weren't created and saved simply to buy a house, raise a family, or to drive around in cars and buy toys. Neither were we saved to be a husband who hates his job but continues to work, doing all he can to provide for his family.

Women were not only created to be wives and mothers and not have any interest or purpose outside of raising a family. Mind you, the only thing my own mother ever wanted to do was to raise children and be a loving wife and mother. But in her later years, she derives her enjoyment in teaching new Christians about God's Word. She has the official sanction by the pastors to do this. She also enjoys proofreading and doing some basic editing of my books. Now that she is not a full-time mother, her hobby would be to sit quietly at her computer and concentrate on her Kingdom work. The added bonus is that she is learning more about God's Word than she ever had time to learn years ago.

As I have earlier mentioned, Kat Kerr has written extensively about Heaven, but she also wrote that if you want to work out what you were born to do, you are to first establish what kind of work brings you the most fulfilment then make a point of doing that. You need not move into doing what you like to do in a full-time capacity, but even doing what turns you on in a part-time capacity will create a purposeful drive to your life.

My Testimony:

About seventeen years ago, I read a book about different personalities. It was such a great book for me to read as I quickly worked out my own personality type. The book also taught me about the kind of work that I would be good at and would be fulfilled in doing. I would rate it among the top five books I have ever read. This book was called "Please Understand Me" and was written by David Kersley. I would highly recommend it to anyone who seriously wants to find their purpose in life.

Apparently, there are sixteen different temperament types that are the subject of the Myers Briggs analysis. I did the suggested test and then went on to read other materials about my type, and I found out a few things that my temperament might be good at. Apparently, people of my type "ENFJ" are great encouragers. They like to see potential in people and champion them to be the best that they can be in life. That sort of sounds what this book you are now reading is all about, doesn't it?

Among other things, the book said that ENFJ's are gifted communicators who can be writers, preachers and pastors. As a writer, I find that I preach, and through Facebook, I seem to give pastoral support to people. I didn't need reminding that I was a good writer as I have forever remembered what my English teacher said when I was only a young lad.

ENFJ's are very intuitive and as a prophet that uses the gift of prophecy, I find that God speaks to me through my intuition and so this is very handy for me in giving prophetic words to people. As a prophet who can give a person a personal message from God, I find that this works well with my talent for encouraging people to be all that they can be.

Another good thing to do is a 'spiritual gifts test' on the Internet. In this test, you will find what you are gifted in to do in life. Some of the things that I score high on are the gift of giving, the gift of poverty (someone who loves to spend all they have to serve God) the gift of encouragement, the gift of teaching and the gift of prophecy. You can see that every spiritual gift that I possess, I am using each week and all that the ENFJ profile says that I would be good at - I am presently doing.

So a key to personal and spiritual fulfilment in your life is to find out what your "temperament" is gifted to do, and also to find out what your "spiritual gifts" are, and to get busy doing what you are naturally good at. I am a people person and so it is no good putting me in a room by myself in a workplace to do filing. There are things that you are born to do and what you are gifted to do, and there is no use doing something that is opposite to that.

I understand that people have bills and daily living expenses, etc and they are stretched in life. But it does not hurt to do a little research on "who you really are" and try and make some plans to start to do what you are gifted in.

It's one thing to find out what your spiritual gifts are, it is quite another thing to organize your life so that all your gifts are being used. So many churches are run by a pastor and a few deacons and no one else seems to get used. It brings much sadness in people who have a gift and yet they are not used by their church. It is one thing to know that you are called to be a preacher but a lot of sadness can come to you if your pastor won't give you the opportunity to preach.

But no matter what is happening in your life, know that God will finish the good work that He started in you. Remember God's promise to you that all things work together for good for those called according to His purpose. If you are sad now, know that Jesus in Heaven is interceding for you to fulfil God's will in your life.

Whilst doors have not opened for me to preach yet, I don't worry so much about that. I keep busy running a group on Facebook, making video teachings, writing and publishing books and serving coffee to the homeless in our Salvation Army community center.

Are you doing what you were born to do, or do you need to do more research? What have you always wanted to do? If time and money were not a problem for you, what would you choose to do with your life? A key to life's fulfilment is discovering and doing that.

God's purpose for you is to be His light to your generation and to bring God's glory with your life. When you find out what you were born to do and you start to do that, make sure you work with the Holy Spirit and you become the best at that, as you can be, because the better you are, the more God will be glorified. If you are called to be a florist, be the best one in your city. If you are called to be a banker, be the most understanding banker in your town. If you are called to be a prophet, be bold and encourage as many people as you can before you are taken up to glory.

As of writing this, I am currently working on four books at once. It's exciting for me each pension payday to be able to put aside some money to go towards one of the many costs of self-publishing, as there are many different processes to produce a book. Can you feel my excitement?

Heavenly Father,

Inspire these people who read this chapter to find out for themselves who they are in Christ, and what they were created to do with their life. I ask that you will fill their lives with joy as they research this topic. In Jesus' name, I ask. Amen.

CHAPTER 9
BEING A "LIGHT" TO OTHERS

This subject speaks about my life's desire. Because Jesus is the light of the world and we are to be like Him, every believer must be forever conscious of reflecting that light. Most of my books would say something about this particular subject as God has strongly reinforced it into my spirit time and time again. Not everyone may read my other books, so I will talk very briefly about being a light in this chapter.

Jesus said: *"You are the light of the world. A city that is set on a hill cannot be hidden. Nor do they light a lamp and put it under a basket, but on a lamp-stand, and it gives light to all who are in the house. Let your light so shine before men, that they may see your good works and glorify your Father in Heaven." Matthew 5:14-16.* Did you pick-up what Jesus called us? He said that we are the "light" of the world.

Jesus is now in Heaven, seated with His Father. All believers in the world-wide church of God are the brothers and sisters of Christ, as we are indwelt by the Holy Spirit. Individually, each believer is to reflect their own unique little light for Jesus and shine like a lamp, but if we humble ourselves enough and we move in the grace of Jesus, the church or the body of Christ is to be like a "city" on a hill.

In Sydney, Australia where I live, two Spirit-led pastor-couple shared a vision - to build a church which would in reality become a city on a hill and to name it Hillsong. Today, Hillsong's music is sung by worshippers around the four corners of the Christian world including Australia, India, China, Korea, the United Kingdom, and almost every other country. Hillsong is not only known for exceptional praise and worship music, but it is also recognized as a training school for other pastors desiring to lead the Body of Christ with excellence. As foundational leaders, God has wonderfully used Brian and Bobby Houston to indeed create a city on a hill which brings light to the world and amazing glory to God.

How can you be a light to your generation? My answer would be: to do the kind of things that Jesus did on earth. For example:

- When someone insults you on Facebook, don't insult them back but turn the other cheek and forgive them. If you feel the need to comment, confront them in private and ask them to account for their action, but give them the chance to apologize. Don't retaliate negatively and then go gossiping about them to others.

- When a person on the streets asks you for spare change, don't lie, but give them at least a dollar because Jesus said to give to everybody who asks of us.

- When someone threatens to take you to court, pay them in full. If possible, we are not to bring dishonor to God's name by going to court. Or when someone asks you for a favor, agree and be prepared to go the extra mile.

In short, we are to be constantly mindful of acting and reacting like Jesus, wherever we go.

If you learn to hear the Holy Spirit and how to prophesy, you can bring an encouraging prophetic word to unbelievers and help lead them closer to Jesus. The way to witness to strangers in the streets via prophecy is taught in my book *"Prophetic Evangelism Made Simple."*

In the past ten years, I have been used to bring a personal prophecy to thousands of people on the streets of my city. Bringing a stranger a much needed word of encouragement by God, or a direction from God without charge and in a simple manner, is a great way to share God's light to others. I want my readers to know that anyone who has the indwelling Holy Spirit within them *can prophesy!* It's a wonderful way to be God's light to this generation.

Simply being constantly aware that you have all the fruit of the Holy Spirit in you will enable you to lovingly share your light with a lost and broken-down world. The nine fruit or "characteristics" of the Holy Spirit are *"love, joy, peace, longsuffering (patience) kindness, goodness, faithfulness, gentleness and self-control."* *Galatians 5:23-24*

Therefore, if you are born-again, you already have all of God's fruit residing within you and by exercising His fruit, the Lord is glorified. He uses His fruit in us to influence and touch people's lives that will lead them closer to saving faith. Jesus spoke about a life that bears much fruit in John 15:1-2. He said: *"I am the true vine, and My Father is the vinedresser. Every branch in Me that does not bear fruit He takes away; and every branch that bears fruit He prunes, that it may bear more fruit."*

People of the world will see this good fruit in us, even though they may not give God the glory. They could just see us as being "nice" people. That's why we need to both "talk-the –walk" as well as to "walk the talk." I say this because some people *are* just naturally nice people, whereas others profess to be Christians and yet display absolutely no visible spiritual fruit. I would say that these people are hypocrites and unless they are truly converted, they will not be in a good place in the final days.

In nature, we all know that fruit trees need to be cut back and pruned regularly in order to grow abundant healthy fruit. Likewise, those of us who do bear God's fruit, the Lord will put to the test and refine us in his refining fire, so that we will bear His fruit more readily.

Trials, persecutions and sufferings are used by the Lord to promote healthy growth. God needs to carve out our character so that we will bear more and more fruit for Him. Bear in mind always that God is far more concerned with developing a godly "character" in us, than He is concerned about developing spiritual gifts in us or making our lives comfortable.

The Apostle Paul wrote a huge part of the New Testament and yet, he suffered far more in his life than most people ever do. Perhaps, the bigger the call of God on one's life, the more suffering will be evidenced within that life. God would need to build a really strong godly character in that person's life. Thankfully, Paul always looked at the greater reward and said: *"For I consider the sufferings of this present time are not worthy to be compared with the glory which shall be revealed in us."* *Romans 8:18*

My Testimony: *At one time in my life, I was extremely prideful. I was right and everyone else was wrong. I was angry, judgemental, and legalistic in all of my theology. At that stage in my life, I was totally unteachable. Years later, I read what God has said about such a person. "A wise son heeds his father's instruction, but a scoffer does not listen to rebuke." Proverbs 13:1. At that time in my life, I had an unteachable spirit and was indeed a scoffer.*

Around this time, God allowed me to be thrust into a cycle of sleeping up to eighteen to twenty hours a day. No matter what time I went to bed, I couldn't get enough sleep. I was just so tired. I slept from 10.00pm to 5.00pm the next day. I would wake up chronically depressed and I would be so tired that around 9.00pm, I would be taking sleeping tablets to get myself back to sleep. This really was sheer torture for me.

The only way I could fight it as a person who suffers with Bipolar Disorder was to stay up all night and not go to bed. I would then stay up all the next day and then stay up all the next night also. In hindsight, I should have sought medical attention. I would deliberately put myself into a state of mania, which is a highly creative state for me and I would write five articles a night besides watching TV. Each article would be about four pages and it would take me quite a while to write.

If I didn't stay up all night and all the next day and all the next night, I would quickly slip right back into the eighteen to twenty hours sleeping again. During the time I suffered this way, I felt my life was not worth living. This pattern went on for four long years and the only way I could get relief and have a normal day or two of happiness and productivity would be to stay up days and nights one after another.

Finally, I received from God a breakthrough: I received a revelation of His incredible grace exhibited in the life, death and resurrection of His Son. I was set free and the pride in my life was gone once and for all.

The Bible exhorts us to humble ourselves, but if we don't do it ourselves, Jesus will do it for us. Therefore, I beg of you, if you have pride issues, get on top of them. You certainly wouldn't want to be put in a fire like the one I went through. Though it was hard at the time to live through, I am so happy that I am the man I am today. I can praise God for the good work that He did in me through this time of agony.

I wish I had a book to be able to give you, with a hundred and one ways you could store up treasures in Heaven and ways for you to shine God's light onto all people. The best I can tell you is to look up the commandments of Jesus and start to obey them in every decision that you make. By walking as Jesus told us to, we will definitely reflect His love to others.

CHAPTER 10
LIVING IN JESUS' PRESENCE

For most of my Christian life, I didn't live in the presence of God. Sure, at times, I would feel God's presence in worship at church on a Sunday, but as to being able to continually walk in the manifest presence of God each day, this certainly wasn't my daily experience. However, about four years ago, my attitude towards God and His Word dramatically changed and I suddenly began to walk in the presence of God each day.

What was different, you may ask? The only way I can explain this phenomena is that I was suddenly very much aware of a wonderful feeling of peace and joy both in my spirit and in my soul area. I knew, without doubt, that Jesus was with me through the power of the Holy Spirit, in a brand new way that I'd never known before. Today, I mostly wake up being conscious of the presence of the Holy Spirit. Perhaps, abiding in Jesus in a deeper way resulted in my being more aware of His presence. Or maybe, it was visa-versa.

Jesus invites us to draw close: *"Abide in Me, and I in you. As the branch cannot bear fruit of itself, unless it abides in the vine, neither can you, unless you abide in Me." John 15:4.* It makes sense that if Jesus is the vine and we are the branches that we can share in a portion of His anointing and this anointing on our life brings with it the manifest presence of God.

I'm not quite sure what I did to deserve this fresh new walk with God, but I know that I am very blessed. I know, even though I walk in the presence, His anointing increases when I pick up my Bible and begin to read it.

The awareness of God's presence also happens to me whenever I read the words of an anointed writer. I feel that everything to do with Jesus seems to increase the power of His presence. Although I spoke earlier about this particular verse, I now feel that it might have more meaning for my reader. Jesus said: *"He who has My commandments and keeps them, it is he who loves Me. And he who loves Me will be loved by My Father, and I will love him and manifest Myself to him." John 14:21*

I think back to my life four years ago, when I first experienced the abiding presence of Jesus and His wonderful peace and joy that simply blew me away. The one major change I had made in my life to cause Jesus to want to hang out with me *was my earnest decision to rest in His "liberating grace power" to follow His commandments.*

Up till then, I had been trying to please God in my own strength. One day, thanks again to the teaching by Andrew Wommack, I finally learnt that Jesus was not impressed with me doing Kingdom work by my own human effort, so all my years of trying to win God's approval had been totally futile. Therefore, I had missed out on much joy in my life.

For believers who suspect that they too, have been trapped into a similar religious mindset, I recommend that you read Chapters 28 and 29 of my book called: *"The Parables of Jesus made simple."* These two chapters are about the new cloth and the new wine. These two short parables taught by Jesus were the result of the disciple's question; as to why their Master did not fast like the religious practice of other spiritual leaders.

"And Jesus said to them, 'Can the friends of the bridegroom mourn as long as the bridegroom is with them? But the days will come when the bridegroom will be taken away from them, and then they will fast. No one puts a piece of un-shrunk cloth on an old garment; for the patch pulls away from the garment, and the tear is made worse. Nor do they put new wine into old wineskins, or else the wineskins break, the wine is spilled, and

the wineskins are ruined. But they put new wine into new wineskins, and both are preserved." Matthew 9:16-17

I have heard that the Gospel of Matthew was primarily written for the Jewish people. The overall theme of this particular Gospel presents Jesus as the long awaited Jewish Messiah who came to fulfil the Jewish Law. There are far more Old Testament quotes in this Gospel than there are in any of the other three Gospels. The Law preserved the Jewish people, but the Law is impossible for man to keep; this truth is reinforced in the New Testament.

The brother of Jesus said: *"For whoever shall keep the whole law, and yet stumble in one point, he is guilty of all." James 2:10.* When the Bible talks about the Law, it's not just referring to the Ten Commandments, but it refers to 313 individual laws found in the first five books of the Old Testament known as "The Torah," which was written by Moses.

The Law pointed to the righteousness and holiness of God. God's chosen people had to experience for themselves the utter futility of trying to reach Heaven's high calling, so that they would readily embrace God's Savior when He came to rescue them. No one can reach Heaven in their own strength. God knew this, as He alone is holy.

This truth is just as relevant today. God loved His precious people and that's why He gave them His impossible laws. He was preparing them to enthusiastically embrace His Own Son as their promised Messiah, who would be able to rescue them from their inherited sinful nature established in the Garden of Eden. Then, in the fullness of time, the Father sent Jesus in all His humility, to fulfil the whole Law for them. But they, in their pride and unbelief, rejected Him, because He didn't resemble the victorious Savior they wanted.

The door to God was then opened up to the gentiles to receive salvation. God still hoped that by doing this, He would provoke the Jews to jealousy and they too would be saved. *"Does this mean that God has rejected His Jewish people forever? Of course not! His purpose was to make His salvation available to the Gentiles, and then the Jews would be jealous and begin to want God's salvation for themselves." Romans 11:11* (Living New Testament)

All Romans Chapter Eleven portrays God's heart for His Jewish people. God dearly loves Israel and He always will. Any nation that does battle against this small nation will ultimately fall, because they will be fighting God. The Bible assures us that Israel's ongoing rejection of their Messiah is not final.

God's covenant with His people will not be broken and His name will be glorified, because He is a covenant-keeping God. The covenant God made with Abraham and his descendents will never be broken by God. We can, therefore, be just as sure that His covenant made with His Bride, the church, is just as secure. Abraham, the Father of Judaism, is also the Father of faith that is seen in the New Testament church.

Jesus summed up the entire Law in just two verses: *"You shall love the Lord your God with all your heart, with all your soul, with all your mind, and with all your strength. This is the first commandment. And the second, like it, is this: 'you shall love your neighbour as yourself!' There is no other commandment greater than these." Mark 12:30-31*

Even harder, Jesus said in John 13:34 *"A new commandment I give to you that you love one another; as I have loved you, that you also love one another."* I ask myself, "would I be willing to be separated from God the Father and die a torturous death on the cross for my neighbor? I would probably excuse myself by saying, "No, by being a mere human, that would be futile, only a perfect human could die for someone else's sins." The point is: God calls us to sacrifice our own personal desires in order to minister His love to others.

My Bible notes explain that this command pushes us beyond our natural human inclinations. Christ's love is not dependent on any quality in us that makes us lovable. He loves because God is love, regardless of our strengths or weaknesses. That thought may be humbling to some who want to be chosen, called, and cherished because of their human credentials of talent, personality, or achievement. However, Christ's kind of love is not motivated by any human qualities, but it is grace-motivated.

If we are to love in His way, we will have to take seriously John 14:14 and ask for this love in Jesus' name. We learn in John 14:16 that the Holy Spirit will do in us what Jesus Himself would have done in us. The Spirit's coming assures continuity with what Jesus did and taught.

For many, many years, I had been very arrogant and disgustingly vocal about the importance of *every believer to obey all the individual commandments of Jesus.* However, in hindsight, my pious belief was unloving and scripturally wrong. Up till four years ago, my religious ego was driven by legalism; I was not in any way motivated by the love and grace of God.

In fact, looking back, I believe that a religious spirit and not the Holy Spirit was the source of my determination to do everything right in the eyes of man, thinking that God would bless me abundantly. Instead of having people flock to me, they were probably running for cover and hoping that they would see me, before I saw them.

Today, as I ponder the changes in my life, I am forever grateful for the amazing love of the Savior for intervening in my life with the New Covenant life-changing revelation of grace. I really do believe that Jesus saw my heart's desire to walk with Him, even though I was not where He wanted me to be in my theology or my behavior at the time. Jesus loved me enough to patiently put aside my foolish pride, because He knew my future destiny.

However, I still firmly believe that abiding in Jesus and being conscious of His commandments has contributed to me experiencing His peace and joy. Because of His goodness and love, Jesus simply wants to bless us because it is His heart to bless all people, especially His believers.

This morning as I led my weekly prophetic class, I had students prophesy over me. A couple of them explained to me that I am swimming deep in the waters of the Holy Spirit. One prophet said I was like a dolphin happily swimming in the sea and that my life is one that is most happy when I am immersed in the Holy Spirit.

From personal experience, I can say that obedience regarding the things of God definitely enables a believer to be more conscious of the Holy Spirit and His desires. This mindset causes us to be able to live in God's presence. Living that way is like your whole life is being immersed in Him. You become more sensitive to the desires and unction of the Holy Spirit and that sensitivity allows you to live in the river of God's glory.

Today, I am not trying to earn God's love in any way. Rather, it is His love and grace that has been unconditionally extended to me that causes me to want to love Him more. I also know that living in God's presence empowers me to withstand attacks directly from the enemy, or by Him working through other people. My life is devoted to spreading the Kingdom of God and bringing knowledge of Him to the people of God. I am giving my all for that cause.

At times, I sleep too much and almost slip back into that awful place where I was trapped for years. On those days, when I wake up very depressed, I find it hard to live in the presence, but on most days, when I am up and about at a regular time, the Holy Spirit comes to hang out with me. If you earnestly want to live in God's presence, I know your prayer will be answered. God's Word assures us: *"Now this is the confidence that we have in Him, that if we ask anything according to His will, He hears us, and if we know that He hears us, whatever we ask, we know that we have the petitions that we have asked of Him. 1 John 5:14-15*

God is the one who gives us both the desire and the ability to shine like lights for Jesus, according to Philippians 2:13-15. God's amazing grace enables us to fulfil His will in our life, but we need to follow His directions and in doing so, we will be abiding in Him. Jesus has promised us: *If you abide in Me, and My words abide in you, you will ask what you desire, and it shall be done for you. John 15:7*

Life is certainly a lot more enjoyable when the presence of God is part of your wakeful existence. Many people go from church to church and conference to conference to live in the presence. Yet, like Moses leading his people through the wilderness, the presence of God actually travels with you in your born-again spirit, every single second of your life. It is my prayer that you discover how to cultivate this awareness of God in your own life.

CHAPTER 11
LIVING IN GOD'S WILL

If we were able to reach a stage in our Christian life where everything we did and said was directed by the Holy Spirit, we would be assured that we were living in the Father's will. It would be truly radical to live in an open Heaven, just like Jesus did on earth.

Paul said: if we choose to follow our past patterns of thinking and behaving, then we are not being led by the Spirit, but by the old dictates of the flesh. He said: *"Therefore brethren, we are debtors - not to the flesh, to live according to the flesh. For if you live according to the flesh you will die; but if by the Spirit you put to death the deeds of the body, you will live. For as many as are led by the Spirit of God, these are sons of God." Romans 8:12-14*

The word "flesh" refers to our soul and body. Paul was not talking about death in a literal sense: neither was he saying that we will lose our salvation if we walk in the flesh. It is the presence of the Holy Spirit in us that qualifies us as being a Son of God. Therefore, to be constantly led by the Holy Spirit is the ultimate goal of every Christian.

Before salvation, we lived continually in the flesh, we had no other option. But now, we can *choose* whether to let our flesh rule, or to act in the power of the Spirit. We can choose to "promote" self or to "die" to self. The more we die to self, the stronger we become spiritually and the more conscious we will be that we are living in God's will.

The Apostle Paul had a godly mindset, because he knew how much God loved him. This was because Jesus radically intervened in his life when he was an overly religious Pharisee. We read about this in Acts Chapter 9:3-19. Saul was renamed "Paul" by Jesus. Saul had been zealously trying to please God by works of the flesh. I was like Saul in the past, because for most of my Christian life, I had been guilty of doing the same "religious" thing.

When I received the revelation of the awesomeness of God's grace, it freed me to be able to walk conscious of the Holy Spirit within me even in the midst of my sin. Although centuries apart, I feel that both Paul and I, along with countless other people, have been trapped in a legalistic mindset, but like Paul, I am so thankful that God's grace intervention caused my entire life to do a back-flip.

When Paul received God's grace revelation deep in his spirit, he totally surrendered his life to Christ. He was truly able to say: *"I have been crucified with Christ, it is no longer I that live, but Christ lives in me; and the life that I now live in the flesh I live by faith in the Son of God, who loved me and gave Himself for me." Galatians 2:20*

Paul saw that sin's power, though "legally" broken, would be "experientially" broken in his life, only when he saw himself on the cross with Jesus. This, too, is to be our revelation. Seeing our self as being crucified with Christ produces good things in our life, instead of our former sin-nature driving us to sin, the *love of Christ* will overwhelm us to the point that we eagerly desire to live our lives for the glory of Jesus. Paul said: *"For the love of God compels us, because we judge thus: that if One died for all, then all died." 2 Corinthians 5:14*

The biblical definition of the word "compel" means that there is a sense of continual "constraint" operating in our lives. Instead of sin once holding us in its tight grip, now Jesus holds us in His firm "love-grip," which prevents us escaping. It is no wonder that Jesus said to His Father: *"Of those whom You gave Me I have lost none." John 18:9*

"If anyone is in Christ, he is a new creation; old things have passed away; behold all things have become new. Now all things are of God, who has reconciled us to Himself through Jesus Christ, and has given us the ministry of reconciliation." 2 Corinthians 5:17-18.

At salvation, we were reconciled to God: we are no longer the person we were. This ministry of reconciliation also gives us the ability to lead others to Christ. 2 Peter 3:9 tells us that God is not willing that *anyone* should perish. He wants everybody to come to repentance and be saved. When we were saved and reconciled to God, we were set free from Satan's firm grip.

"You were dead in sins, and your sinful desires were not yet cut away. Then He gave you a share in the very life of Christ, for He forgave all your sins, and blotted out the charges proved against you, the list of His commandments which you had not obeyed. He took this list of sins and destroyed it by nailing it to Christ's cross. In this way God took away Satan's power to accuse you of sin, and God openly displayed to the whole world Christ's triumph at the cross where your sins were all taken away." Colossians 2:13-15 – Living New Testament

The punishment for all sin had been placed onto Jesus. It's Satan who wants to condemn us - he is our accuser. (Revelation 12:10) We are to rejoice like Paul: *"For the law of the Spirit of life in Christ Jesus has made me free from the law of sin and death." Romans 8:2.* What could not be done by human effort has been done through the power of the Holy Spirit.

To the believer, Satan is actually a toothless tiger, he has been stripped of his powerful bite and he must retreat at our command in Jesus' Name to depart from us. Satan only has power if we open the door to him. Because all our sins, past, present and future, was heaped onto the body of Jesus on the cross, the wrath and holiness of the Father has been fully appeased.

Before the cross, failure to obey the Law brought on the curse of the Law, but Christ has forever redeemed us from this curse. He *became* the curse and He dissolved it. *"Christ has redeemed us from the curse of the law, having become a curse for us." Galatians 3:13a*

Therefore: *Walk in the Spirit, and you shall not fulfil the lust of the flesh" Galatians 5:16.* But how can we do this? We not only war against wrong programming since birth, but we also war against constant onslaughts by Satan and his demonic representatives, who keep dropping sinful thoughts into our mind.

Thankfully, God gave Paul the answer to this massive problem, he said: *"For though we walk in the flesh, we do not war according to the flesh. For the weapons of our warfare are not carnal (fleshly) but mighty in God for pulling down strongholds, casting down arguments and every high thing that exalts itself against the knowledge of God, bringing every thought into captivity."* 2 Corinthians 10:3-5.

I couldn't understand this passage when I was a young Christian, then gradually over time, I realized that walking in the Spirit is achieved *"by us constantly taking our thoughts captive."* This means that we are to only act on the thought if it sits right with our born-again spirit. Understanding God's Word is, therefore, vital for us to be able to do this. If the Word of God is contrary to the thought, we should rebuke it, dismiss it and go on with our life.

Our minds are constantly bombarded with negative thoughts; for example: someone starts a nasty argument on Facebook and insults you. What should you do? Okay, Jesus says to forgive, but He also says to confront a person who has offended you *privately,* and give them the opportunity to see their error and to ask you to forgive them. If they refuse to admit they have done wrong, we are to forgive them and then turn the other cheek. If they repent, we are to forgive them and we have also restored the relationship which brings God glory.

The Word of God certainly doesn't say that we are to publicly call them out on Facebook. This is just one example of taking every thought captive. This is still a work in progress for me personally, as I have not yet perfected this ideal reaction.

I will try to simplify this "thought-captive" process. Before every sin we commit, a thought had already entered our mind. Walking in the Spirit is habitually taking that thought captive, and not acting on it until the prompting of the Holy Spirit assures us that it's the right thing to do. If the Holy Spirit or the Word of God convicts us in any way, we must rebuke the thought and not allow it to rule us anymore. The brother of Jesus has given us the typical process that leads to all sin. James said the following:

"Blessed is the man who endures temptation; for when he has been approved, he will receive the crown of life which the Lord has promised to those who love Him. Let no one say when he is temped, 'I am tempted by God' for God cannot be tempted by evil, nor does He Himself tempt anyone. But each one is tempted when he is drawn away by his own desires and enticed. Then, when desire has conceived, it gives birth to sin; and sin, when it is full-grown, brings forth death. Do not be deceived, my beloved brethren." James 1:12-16

We need to realize that Satan is actually behind all attacks on us and if we react badly, it means we have given him temporary control over our life and we forfeit our joy.

Paul says: *"Let him who is taught the word share in all good things with him who teaches. Do not be deceived, God is not mocked; for whatever a man sows, that he will also reap. For he who sows to his flesh will of the flesh reap corruption, but he who sows to the Spirit will of the Spirit reap everlasting life. And let us not grow weary while doing good, for in due season we shall reap if we do not lose heart. Therefore, as we have opportunity, let us do good to all, especially to those who are of the household of faith.* Galatians 6:6-10

We know that we are to give to the poor and to the widows, but here, we are told to give to our spiritual instructors. This passage assures us that God is not mocked. (The word "mock" in Greek means to turn up the nose or to sneer.) We are to know that what we do with our money produces either positive or negative consequences in the spiritual realm. Therefore, the more we sow to the Spirit, the easier it will become. *Our life will see favor and rewards.*

In the meantime, Paul encourages us not to grow weary in doing good towards others. You might have been serving the Lord for many years in a way that has been quite taxing at times. You are eager to see promotion, or to perhaps see a reward for what you have done. Paul says not to lose heart, for one day, you will reap a harvest. We are to particularly look after our brothers and sisters in the Lord.

We are not saved by works, but once saved, we will naturally engage in good works because we want to be obedient to God and to glorify Him in our life. Therefore, it's very important that soon after salvation, Believer's Baptism should occur. This baptism is not for the unsaved or for a very young child. This baptism is a deliberate act of obedience to the command of Jesus because it is a public witness to our friends and family to the reality of what Christ has already done in our lives.

Believer's Baptism is for Christians only. It is the physical re-enactment of what invisibly took place in the unseen "spiritual realm" at the point of salvation, when we were spiritually baptized into Christ. To be fully immersed in water at our public baptism physically portrays *"our spiritual death and burial"* while rising up out of the water physically portrays *"our new spiritual union"* with the Risen Savior. (See Romans 6:3-4)

Salvation is freely given to us, but it came at enormous cost to God! We are not to treat our freedom lightly. *"For you brethren, have been called to liberty; only do not use liberty as an opportunity for the flesh, but through love serve one another. For all the law is fulfilled in one word, even in this: "You shall love your neighbour as yourself." Galatians 5:13-14*

We have freedom in Christ to live a life where we can be forgiven and washed clean each time we fall. But we must not use the grace of God in a way where we have a license to sin. We should not use our freedom in Christ to choose to live in the flesh, but in all things, we should follow the Word of God and the leadings of the Holy Spirit.

For many years, I had focused on "doing" things to please God, but worse still, I pushed my opinions onto everybody else. One of the many verses that released freedom and liberty to me was: *"The sting of death is sin, and the strength of sin is the law."1 Corinthians 15:56.*

Up till that point, I had been focused on trying to keep the Laws of God, but suddenly, I realized that the Law only strengthened the power of sin to rule in my life, making me feel trapped and defeated. When I began to center my focus on the empowerment of God's grace, it gave me the power to break sin's hold on me. In other words, I discovered that the more sin-conscious I was, the more I sinned. In contrast, the more grace-conscious I became, the less I sinned. For years, I had my theology back-to-front and the devil was having a field day in my life.

Actually, we know that the Law promotes sin, for example: if you entered a room and saw a sign: "Don't touch – wet paint" in front of a desk, what would be the very first thing you would do? You would purposely go and touch that desk, wouldn't you? If the sign had not been there, you would have probably ignored the desk. The "Do Not" sign provoked you to touch it, and that is exactly what God's Law does: *it provokes us to break it!*

We know that being able to do everything that the Holy Spirit tells us to do each day would be living in God's will. The commandments of Jesus are simply a detailed way of loving God and our fellow man. We also know that if we catch every thought and judge it according to Scripture and then act accordingly, we would be walking in the Spirit.

Jesus wants us to put into practice the things He has taught. He also gave a scary warning when He said: *"Therefore whoever hears these sayings of Mine, and does them, I will liken him to a wise man who built his house on the rock: and the rain descended, the floods came, and the winds blew and beat on that house; and it did not fall, for it was founded on the rock. But everyone who hears these sayings of Mine, and does not do them, will be like a foolish man who built his house on the sand: and the rain descended, the floods came, and the winds blew and beat on that house; and it fell. And great was its fall." Matthew 7:24-27*

Some believers may be unaware that there is a coming storm-threat that may threaten to crush their house. Scripture reveals that as the world becomes increasingly darker, leading up to Christ's return, some people may experience a very real storm. In such a time, they will need to call out to God, the mighty anchor for their soul. (Hebrews 6:19)

If we do get caught in the coming worldwide storms, we will need to stand on the promises of God, e.g. *"You will keep him in perfect peace, whose mind is stayed on You." Isaiah 26:3. "Be anxious for nothing, but in everything by prayer and supplication, with thanksgiving, let your requests be made known to God and the peace of God, which surpasses all understanding, will guard your hearts and minds through Christ Jesus." Philippians 4:6-7*

If the passage in Matthew 7:24-27 is taken literally by my readers, you need to learn how to walk in the Holy Spirit and judge every thought by what God's commandments say to do, so you will be kept safe through the coming worldwide storms. If you theologically disagree with me, I pray also that you will be safe in the coming trials that are ahead.

CHAPTER 12
HEARING JESUS SPEAK

I cannot even begin to imagine how anyone could live the Christian life without hearing the voice of Jesus speaking to them. As I think back, Jesus has been speaking to me since I was converted at the age of eight. I believe that being able to hear His voice is the prime reason why I have been able to maintain my faith, even though many of my actions in the past have definitely not been God glorifying! If you are a born-again believer and you do not hear Jesus speaking to you, I want you to know that this problem can be solved. Our Good Shepherd assures us that we are meant to hear His voice.

> Jesus said: *"Most assuredly, I say to you, he who does not enter the sheepfold by the door, but climbs up some other way, the same is a thief and a robber. But he who enters by the door is the shepherd of the sheep. To him the doorkeeper opens, and the sheep hear his voice; and he calls his own sheep by name and leads them out. And when he brings out his own sheep, he goes before them; and the sheep follow him, for they know his voice. Yet they will by no means follow a stranger, but will flee from him, for they do not know the voice of strangers. Jesus used this illustration, but they did not understand the things which He spoke to them. Then Jesus said to them again, 'Most assuredly, I say to you, I am the door of the sheep. All who ever came before Me are thieves and robbers, but the sheep did not hear them."* John 10:1-8

Jesus says that He is the "door" to the sheepfold. His sheep are to hear His voice as He leads them out of the sheepfold. *Jesus wants us to hear Him.* Living for eternity includes living with the love and edification of the One that holds eternity in His hands. Jesus not only wants to speak to us, He says He calls us by name;

He wants to lead us and bring us comfort. I discovered that when you begin to hear Jesus, it's beneficial to ask Him to use your name each time He speaks to you, so that you know He is speaking, rather than your own thoughts.

Bear in mind, Jesus rarely speaks to people in an audible voice. His voice has always been just a thought within my spirit. I have trained myself to be in an attitude of listening for Him, so I believe that I've heard Him each time He has spoken to me. With further practice, you will not only be able to hear the voice of Jesus, but you will be able to intuitively recognize the voice also of the Father and the Holy Spirit. After years of such training, I can now live in relationship with the whole three of the Godhead and they all speak to me when they need to.

Part of successful living is to live with a great relationship with our Creator. Therefore, it's so important to know that Jesus wants to speak to you. His desire is to have a prominent role in your everyday life: He wants to lead you step-by-step. That's why we have been instructed in Proverbs 3:4-5 to: *Trust in the Lord with all your heart, and lean not on your own understanding; in all your ways acknowledge Him, and He shall direct your paths."*

Jesus has many things He wants to say, yet so often, people don't take the time to listen. They block out His voice just by being busy and focused on their own agenda. There would be just so many comforting words and advice He has for all of us, yet when we do spend time with Him, mostly, we are the ones who do all the talking. It must sadden Him to know that His own redeemed family don't take delight in His Company, but would rather fill their mind with less important things.

Jesus is truly the very best friend anyone could possibly have. He delights in being our Great Shepherd: our provider; our protector and closest friend. In fact, He wants us to enjoy the same close relationship with Him and with His Father that He experienced on earth. Before going to the cross, Jesus especially took time to be alone with His Father, not to just pray for strength Himself, but to plead protection over us and all future believers.

Chapter 17 emphasizes the miracle of oneness. My Bible notes teach that the equation of oneness is profound, and yet very simple: one plus one plus one equals one; Christ, ourselves, and another believer, equals oneness. It is Christ in our brother or sister who reaches out to the Christ in us. We are united in and through Him; this is one of the many miracles of the indwelling Christ.

Early in His intercessory prayer to His Father, Jesus said: *"And this is eternal life, that they may know You, the only true God, and Jesus Christ whom You have sent. I have glorified You on the earth. I have finished the work which You have given Me to do?" John 17:3-4*

Obviously, Jesus hadn't yet died for our sins, so exactly what was the particular "work" that His Father had given Him to do on earth? The answer is found in John's previous chapter. Here, we see that Jesus had been preparing His disciples for His departure, by reassuring them that He would send the Holy Spirit to be their personal trainer and guide. He confided to His disciples, *"The Father Himself loves you because you have loved Me, and have believed that I came forth from God. I came forth from the Father and have come into the world. Again, I leave the world and go to the Father." John 16:27-28*

Up till then, many of the words of Jesus had puzzled His friends: His words were hard to discern and their hearing had seemed dull but now, suddenly, His words impacted their spirit and unlocked the mystery surrounding their Master. *"His disciples said to Him, 'See, now You are speaking plainly, and using no figure of speech! Now we are sure that You know all things, and have no need that anyone should question You. By this we believe that You came forth from God.'" John 16:29-30*

"Jesus answered them, 'Do you now believe?'"John 16:31 He went on to assure them that they would soon scatter from Him but His Father would be with Him. He reinforced to them that His peace and their belief in Him would hold them securely, regardless of the circumstances they would soon be facing.

After three years of close fellowship with Jesus, His disciples had finally received personal spiritual revelation and understood with their mind, and deep in their spirit, the true identity of their Master, and why His teachings and actions were so radically different to anyone else.

Now, for the first time, the disciples realized that: *God the Father had sent Jesus to earth to reveal the Father's extraordinary love for them and for all mankind. In fact, I believe that this was the "work" that the Father had commissioned Jesus to do on earth.*

To come to the knowledge that we are deeply loved by God the Father is truly liberating news, for it proves that the devil is a liar and deceiver. More importantly, such knowledge triggers in our soul area the desire to respond to God's extravagant kind of love. It encourages us to do everything we can to please Him, not in order to impress Him or to receive rewards in Heaven, but as an act of practical thanksgiving and worship to Him.

These words of Jesus would have prompted Philip to remember an earlier conversation. He had asked Jesus to show him the Father and Jesus had replied *"Have I been with you so long, and yet you have not known Me, Philip? He who has seen Me has seen the Father, so how can you say, 'Show us the Father'? Do you not believe that I am in the Father, and the Father in Me? The words that I speak to you I do not speak on My own authority; but the Father who dwells in Me does the works. Believe Me that I am in the Father and the Father in Me, or else believe Me for the sake of the works themselves." John 14:9-11*

For three years, the disciples had been highly privileged to listen intently to the voice of Jesus. His words were unique and they loved to listen to Him. They had personally witnessed His incredible love and grace to all He met. In fact, the only people who had ever upset their Master had been the hypercritical Pharisees and the traders in His Father's house of prayer.

Now, finally, the disciples realized for the first time that the awesome "I AM" in Heaven whom they had worshipped under Judaism, and Jesus their Master were "One" in every way.

Since their first meeting with Jesus, He had displayed a wondrously, favorable impression of the Father's characteristics to all who sought Him. He was the physical representation of His Father, yet even more incredible, both the Father and Jesus truly loved them regardless of their weaknesses. This revelation truth is to be openly shared with the whole world.

The "work on earth" His Father had sent Him to do was done and it was time now to draw strength and assurance from His Father in order to tackle His reconciliation assignment. Soon after His prayerful solitude in the Garden, Jesus "glorified" the Father by calmly subjecting Himself to the spiritual separation and the mental and physical agony of the cross. By doing so, *He completed His incredible "assignment" on earth.* Therefore, His triumphant final words were: *"'It is finished!' And bowing His head, He gave up His spirit." John 19:30*

Jesus successfully completed a dual task. What, then, is our work and assignment on earth?

Our work: Before the Cross, the disciples had asked Jesus, *"What shall we do, that we may work the works of God?* He replied: *"This is the work of God that you believe in Him whom He sent." John 6:29.* Today, the "work" of every believer is to go on believing in Jesus. Regardless of what is happening in the world or in our lives, we are to keep looking to Him for nothing is too difficult for Him to handle. We need to develop the mindset of listening to His voice and to ignore the negative voices of the world.

Our assignment: The Father through Jesus, has called, chosen, justified, equipped and anointed the Bride of Christ to glorify God on earth and to reconcile people to Him through Christ. Our assignment is "The Great Commission" – believers are to be a living example of Jesus on earth, in word and action by passing on to others His Father's love for them.

Our special assignment was given to us by Jesus: *"Go therefore and make disciples of all the nations, baptizing them in the name of the Father and of the Son and of the Holy Spirit, teaching them to observe all things that I have commanded you; and lo, I am with you always, even to the end of the age. Amen."* Matthew 28:19-20

Just like our parents helped us with homework assignments, God's Holy Spirit helps us in our assignment of "glorifying God" in our everyday life. Jesus gave us an almost impossible task. He said: *"A new commandment I give to you, that you love one another, as I have loved you, that you also love one another."* John 13:34.

To obey this commandment, we need to rely on the presence and power of the Holy Spirit in us. God intervened in our life because of His love, mercy and grace. Therefore, we are to reach others with His love, mercy and grace. We need only to ask for God's wisdom and to trust in the fruit of the Holy Spirit abiding in us, which is: *"love, joy, peace, longsuffering, kindness, goodness, faithfulness, gentleness and self-control."* Galatians 5:22-23

After Jesus rose from the dead, He visited His disciples and they were given more details of their assignment. Jesus said them, *"Go into all the world and preach the gospel to every creature. He who believes and is baptized will be saved; but he who does not believe will be condemned. And these signs will follow those who believe; In My name they will cast out demons; they will speak with new tongues; they will take up serpents; and if they drink anything deadly, it will by no means hurt them, they will lay hands on the sick, and they will recover." Mark 16:15-18*

Jesus was not saying here that if you are not "water baptized" you will be condemned. Water baptism is the physical "replay" *of our original spiritual baptism into the body of Christ* - Jesus is the Head and every believer is part of His body. This spiritual baptism occurred when you asked Jesus into your heart. That's why Paul says in his epistles that we are "in" Christ.

Years ago, if I'd been asked: Why did Jesus come to earth?" I probably would have spoken about original sin and its consequences and the fact that unless we turn to Jesus, we will be separated forever from our Creator. Of course, all that is true, but we tend to just see things from our own human perspective and not from our loving Father's point of view.

When we see God's plan for mankind from His perspective, we realize that right from the beginning, God wanted a perfect and beautiful bride who would love Him forever and whom He could love and cherish for all eternity. But on earth, our oldest ancestors exercised their free-will by choosing to believe the lie of the devil rather than the truth of God.

Because God loved us so much, the Father chose to solve the problem, even though it would cost Him His Own Son. He sent Jesus to purchase forever His beautiful "bride" and to one day bring her back to live for all eternity with Him. The Gospel is the greatest "true love story" imaginable, yet so many people are either ignorant of it, or they are offended by it.

What is eternal life? Eternal life is found in a person. John the Apostle said: *"This is the testimony; that God has given us eternal life, and this life is in His Son. He who has the Son has life; he who does not have the Son of God does not have life." I John 5:11-12.* Therefore, the instant we receive Jesus as our own personal Savior, "eternal life" comes into our life.

God has always been speaking to His people. He had called His prophet, Hosea, to give His Jewish people a special promise: *"I will ransom them from the power of the grave. I will redeem them from death."* Hosea 13:14. Also, in Isaiah Chapter 53, we find God's detailed rescue plan. Over seven hundred years later, Jesus died on the cross and rose victoriously from the grave. Death for the believer has lost its sting because God's plan has come to pass.

We all have plans in life. For example: We know that every grand building ever built, first had a plan drawn-up by a skilled architect. A builder studied that plan and built his project to the specifications set down by the architect. In the same way, God is the designer of our life and He certainly has His unique plan for it, already set down. As the builders of our life, it's important that that we build it according to God's plan set down before the foundations of the earth. Jesus wants to guide us on our set-down life journey. It's vital that we learn to hear Him and to live from a place where we are in constant communion with Him.

My Testimony: I am used to listening to the voice of Jesus. I have trained myself over years to do this. As I shared earlier in Chapter 2, He has been using my listening ability to write books and self-publish them. It has opened up a whole new life for me.

When you have the mindset to be always listening for God to speak, you will not be disappointed. The Holy Spirit will start to speak to you and direct you. Jesus directs me in all sorts of ways. I am very much aware that He always gives me things to say to strangers, whenever I exercise the gift of prophecy the Holy Spirit has given me. My Lord Jesus is a wonderful friend, because He lovingly understands me completely.

Jesus wants to be part of your everyday life so He wants to speak to you. He doesn't want this book to become just another "nice" book that you read and put down. He wants you to exercise faith in Him and take positive action to apply His godly principles into your life. Christ Jesus is to take up His rightful place as the chief cornerstone in your life. The Apostle Peter referred to Isaiah 28:16 when he penned these words concerning the Messiah: *"Behold, I lay in Zion a chief cornerstone, elect, precious, and he who believes on Him will by no means be put to shame." 1 Peter 2:6*

To the unbeliever, Jesus - God's "cornerstone, "*is a stumbling stone and a rock of offense"*. Also, we are told that: *"the message of the cross is foolishness to those who are perishing, but to us who are being saved it is the power of God." Romans 9:33 and 1 Corinthians 1:18*

Lord Jesus wants to bless us in every way and as our Good Shepherd, He wants to come off the pages of the Bible, so as to write chapters in our book of life with us. Yes, Jesus wants be everyone's Savior and Lord, but He also wants to be our constant Friend and Counselor.

As I have said before, *"Inside Out Training and Equipping School"* on Facebook is a place where you can be taught how to hear the voice of Jesus. On this site, you will even be taught how to hear from God for others and bless them with prophecy. This will draw them closer to Jesus. You may not want to stay and be part of all their courses, but do yourself a favor - *don't just read this paragraph and say*, 'that's a good suggestion' and do nothing further.

I know that we all want to enjoy an exciting and successful Christian life. I also assume that every believer wants to enter eternity with the best preparation possible. One success key is to have the ability to be continually led by Jesus, by hearing the Good Shepherd's voice.

When questioned by His disciples, Jesus spoke of end time events in Matthew Chapter 24, Mark Chapter 13, and Luke Chapter 21. *"And Jesus, answering them, began to say: 'Take heed that no one deceives you. For many will come in My name, saying 'I am He,' and will deceived many" Mark 13:5-6*

"For false christs and false prophets, will rise and show great signs and wonders to deceive, if possible, even the elect." Matthew 24:24-25. The present day "elect" of God is the universal Bride of Christ, yet Jesus inferred that if possible, even the elect could be deceived.

Jesus as our Good Shepherd reassured His disciples: *"All that the Father gives Me will come to Me, and the one who comes to Me I will by no means cast out." John 6:37.* Later, when Jesus knew His time had come, He prayed alone to His Father for the ongoing protection for all His future believers. He wants us to have the same relationship with His Father that He enjoyed whilst on earth. He certainly didn't want the evil one to lead any of His elect astray. Before He completed His assignment, He had prayed to His Father: *"Sanctify them by Your truth, Your word is truth." John 17:17.*

Today, Jesus is not physically here, but we have the completed Word of God to equip us to glorify the Father. Also, we have the Holy Spirit within us to enable us to understand God's Word. Therefore, we are fully equipped to know the will of God in our life.

Jesus had warned His disciples that there is going to come a time when there will be many false teachers and false voices rising up to lead people away from the right Source. In that day, you will need to hold firm to sound Biblical doctrine, so as to warn others of any false information. To do that, you will need to be personally familiar with God's Word and be able to recognize the anointing of Jesus, in the voices of teachers who you listen to and obey. If you are not scripturally prepared in this way, how are you going to react to false teaching by others, or how are you going to assist others not to be deceived?

For many years, I was seriously misled in my doctrine, even though I truly loved the Lord. Therefore, I know that some false teachers are totally ignorant that they are being led into error by demons. I have always had great passion to lead others to Christ, but the devil had me so bound-up in Old Testament legalism, that instead of showing mercy and grace to my Christian brothers and sisters, I would loudly and zealously argue my case. Thankfully, God knew my heart, He knew I wasn't deliberately trying to stifle God's grace in my theology. However, many false teachers will appear to be sincerely loving and genuine, so that you will believe their twisted interpretation of Scripture.

Tell me, if you don't take steps to recognize the voice of Jesus right now, how are you going to be safe during the perilous times ahead? I don't want to scare you because I know that scare tactics rarely work. I say this, because it was prophesied by Jesus in the last days that many false "christs" would arise and deceive many people. It has also been prophesied that before the end, there will be a great falling away.

> Paul says: *"Let no one deceive you by any means; for that Day will not come unless the falling away comes first, and the man of sin is revealed, the son of perdition... the coming of the lawless one is according to the working of Satan, with all power, signs, and lying wonders."* 2 Thessalonians 2: 3 and 9

I personally believe that the falling away has already begun. People may not want to deny Christ Jesus, or walk away from Christianity, but they may be led away from Jesus by someone who actually claims to be Him. I don't want any of my readers to be deceived like this. Today is not the time to be lazy and put off learning to hear the voice of Jesus. It's not the time to put this book on the shelf and say, "I'll do that another time." It is time to go to Facebook and in the search bar, to look up the group I have mentioned a number of times now, and begin to hear Jesus talk to you.

CHAPTER 13

WALKING BY THE HOLY SPIRIT

Even though I have already spoken on this subject, I feel I need to explore it a little more. If we can walk by the Holy Spirit each and every day, then we would have a good life and we would bless many people. First, let's have a look at what the Apostle Paul says about sin.

> *"Now I, Paul, myself am pleading with you by the meekness and gentleness of Christ—who in presence am lowly among you, but being absent am bold toward you. But I beg you that when I am present I may not be bold with that confidence by which I intend to be bold against some, who think of us as if we walked according to the flesh. For though we walk in the flesh, we do not war according to the flesh. For the weapons of our warfare are not carnal but mighty in God for pulling down strongholds, casting down arguments and every high thing that exalts itself against the knowledge of God, bringing every thought into captivity to the obedience of Christ, and being ready to punish all disobedience when your obedience is fulfilled."* 2 Corinthians 10:1-6

It isn't a sin to have a wrong thought. I say this, because Satan and his minions drop negative thoughts into our mind all the time. However, a wrong thought becomes sin when we dwell on it, instead of casting it aside. Paul told us to take our thoughts "captive" and compare it to what Jesus wants us to do. If we believe that our thought lines up with God's Word, then we can act on it. But if on reflection, the thought is contrary to God's will, we should dismiss it as not being worthy. Even if the thought comes back, which it often will, we should be quick to dismiss it and deliberately think of something more worthy.

Jesus, the Holy Spirit or the Father will often place a thought into our mind. This thought, too, should be weighed with Scripture. By doing this, we are deliberately building godly new tracks in our brain's thought- pattern process and this is all part of the ongoing sanctification work to be carried out in our soul area. When we have established that the thought is of God, then we can transfer that thought into the required godly action.

As we learn to be open to listen to Jesus and the Holy Spirit, we will often receive leadings and suggestions. We are to discern these suggestions and to do them. Some of the directions may call for urgent action while others may require us to take action at some point down the line. God will often give us a vision and a plan He has for us years in advance. Therefore, it's important to learn what is needed now and what is being spoken about in the future.

Some say that it's too hard to resist sinful thoughts. These people may be trapped in sinful addictions like I had been. For these people, the following verse should be of comfort - *"No temptation has overtaken you except such as is common to man; but God is faithful, who will not allow you to be tempted beyond what you are able, but with the temptation will also make the way of escape, that you may be able to bear it."* 1 Corinthians 10:13.

This verse may initially annoy the reader, because they have tried to resist temptation and have failed miserably. However, God's Word assures us that nothing is too difficult for God and you need to keep on reminding yourself that God's Word is powerful for breaking negative mindsets and the like. I would suggest that you declare out loud so that the enemy can hear: *"I can do all things through Christ who strengthens me"* Philippians *4:13.* I say this because it is an overcoming technique that I repeatedly do, to assist me to combat many trials, not only temptation in my soul area, but physical pain as well.

Human strength is very weak when it comes to temptation, but we must always be mindful that every believer has the same power in them that raised Jesus from the dead. We therefore must rest in God's ability within us. We know that *"God is able to do exceedingly abundantly above all that we ask or think, according to the power that works in us." Ephesians 3:20.* The power in us is God Himself, so dwell on His miracle-working power working within you, and not on your own fleshly weakness.

Bear in mind too, that a demon of lust or perversion may be involved. If this is the case, freedom from the sin may not be able to happen until that believer has sought out and received deliverance. I know that after deliverance, I had victory over my addictive sins.

The greatest revelation I have ever received apart from salvation itself was to truly discover that I was much loved by God, *despite the besetting sin that plagued me.* My prayer would be that every reader would have the same revelation that God's love towards us is unconditional. We are to know that it's the devil that brings condemnation onto us, not the Holy Spirit.

From the moment of salvation to when we meet Jesus, believers are on a constant journey with God: we are a "work in progress" until God takes us home to Heaven. To me, a physical example of this kind of work is when I look at major road works. For months on end, we can drive along a particular highway and see massive road works being carried out and the whole area looks like one gigantic mess.

We know that there has been someone who has designed the finished product and has set plans on paper for every part of the project. Every workman is under orders to do their specific part. But when I pass by, I have no idea how the mess is going to be resolved or what the final work will look like. I just have to rest in the fact that some brilliant designer will eventually showcase his work for all to see. I say this because God already sees the finished work in us, that's why He's not appalled by any mess in our lives.

In the meantime, He focuses His attention on His Holy Spirit in us. The mess in our life has been created either directly by the devil, or indirectly by our wrong choices or by the wrong choices of others. Although the "mess" in our life is not God's perfect will, He will use it to bring His perfect will into reality. He doesn't want us bound in sin, because He loves us and wants to see us free from the burden that is causing us grief and guilt.

As someone who has had much "mess" in their life, I can personally testify that I couldn't see any lasting freedom until I accepted the fact that Jesus is constantly crazy about me, even in the midst of my sin. When that revelation came to me, I had my wonderful breakthrough. Ask God to give you a personal revelation of His awesome love for you.

We know that Jesus often hung around with the so-called scum of society and these people loved Him. He was known as the friend of prostitutes and tax collectors. These people had a bad reputation but Jesus gladly embraced them. In fact, Matthew, a former tax-collector, became one of the disciples of Jesus and was used by God to write one of the four Gospels. Tax collectors in those days were mostly extortionists who pocketed extra tax for their own personal use. The "righteous" religious Pharisees despised these sinners.

> *"Now it happened, as Jesus sat at the table in the house, that behold, many tax collectors and sinners came and sat with Him and His disciples. And when the Pharisees saw it, they said to the disciples, 'Why does your Teacher sit with tax collectors and sinners?' When Jesus heard that He said to them: 'Those who are well have no need for a physician, but those who are sick. But go and learn what this means: I desire mercy and not sacrifice, for I did not come to call the righteous, but sinners to repentance.'"* Matthew 9:10-13

The only people who Jesus cannot save are those who continually pride themselves as being self-righteous and self-sufficient as Jesus came to save professed sinners. The Pharisees, who were pious religious leaders at the time, saw themselves as being "above" everyone else. They were self-focused and were continually judgmental of others. They had no mercy. Instead, they boasted about their religious sacrifices. Jesus said: *"Woe to you scribes and Pharisees, hypocrites! For you are like whitewashed tombs which indeed appear beautiful outwardly, but inside are full of dead men's bones and all uncleanness." Matthew 23:24*

Mercy and compassion demonstrates kindness, empathy or charity toward someone who is in need. Compassion is something that is first felt and then acted upon with mercy. Jesus is the supreme example of such a person as He took our need and sin upon Himself. Compassion is seeing a need whilst mercy is fulfilling that need. Another example of compassion and mercy is in Matthew 14:14: *"And when Jesus went out He saw a great multitude; and He was moved with compassion for them, and healed their sick."* Later, Jesus miraculously fed them as He knew they had nothing to eat and needed strength for their long journey back home.

If you feel "stuck" in sin, know that freedom is possible, because like me, there is a way of escape for you. I only found freedom from my sinful habit when I came to realize that I could not beat it in my own strength and by my own efforts. I had to rest in the grace and power of God to beat it. As I have said, the catalyst for my freedom was discovering that *God loved me even in my sin.* This liberating revelation severely weakened Satan's hold on me for I had wrongly believed in Satan's lies, about "the conditional" love of God for many years.

God's grace is a favor that He bestowed on us at salvation. His grace is also a force or power that we are to release to others, including ourselves: *"Of His fullness we have all received, and grace for grace. For the law was given through Moses, but grace and truth came through Jesus Christ" John 1:16-17.* Listed below, I have briefly summarized points taken from John Bevere's book:

"Extraordinary Grace". (I recommend you read this book.)

1.   God's grace is an unmerited gift given at our salvation. Faith in His grace is also the basis for our ongoing ability to please God. The more we choose to walk in God's grace, the more His peace and grace is multiplied in our life.

2.   God's love towards us is "unconditional" because His love is based on *His own character and faithfulness,* not on our character and faithfulness as the devil suggests.

3.   Satan's worst fear is for us to discover the full power of God's grace because he wants to keep us in bondage. No longer are we struggling sinners, we are much more: *"Beloved, now we are children of God"* 1 John 3:2. God's makeup is *now* part of us.

4.   Grace not only credits us with Christ's righteousness - it overcomes our helplessness to live a God-pleasing lifestyle. *"For the grace of God that brings salvation has appeared to all men, teaching us that, denying ungodliness and worldly lusts, we should live soberly, righteously, and godly in the present age."* Titus 2:11-12 God's grace power enables us to live a godly life.

5.   We are taught that in Heaven we will be like Jesus but *1 John 4:17* says *"As He is, so are we in this world."* Grace not only covers sin, but it gives us ongoing power to resist sin. How? Because the Father now sees us covered by the blood of His Son.

6.   God's Grace is to be a spiritual tool for us to use. If we believe we are just sinners saved by grace, we will live like sinners. Good and bad seeds are planted by words of

others or by our own mouth, but as we confess God's words over our life, we'll renew our mind and live in victory.

7.   Grace gives us power to live the Christian life and mercy keeps us free from guilt, condemnation and shame, all of which try to pull us back into sin's grip. Mercy is given for our failures i.e. our sins that we've repented of. Grace is given to help and to empower us. *"Let us come boldly to the throne of grace that we may obtain mercy and find grace to help in time of need." Hebrews 4:16*

We are told *not to receive God's grace in vain.* (2 Corinthians 6:1) Therefore, *we are to cleanse ourselves from all filthiness.* (2 Corinthians 7:1) At salvation, the blood of Jesus cleansed us from all sins. Remember, we had no part in this process; but now in sanctification, *we are to co-operate with* God *to moment by moment cleanse ourselves.* God supplies the necessary empowerment of grace to clean, *but we are to do the actual hard scrubbing.*

For most of my life, I had been taught that I had both a sin nature and a new nature. It was explained that "the nature I fed the most would be the nature that surfaced the most." That explanation made perfect sense to me, until I really came to understand Romans Chapter Six.

Here, I discovered that a believer no longer has a sin nature. Since salvation, I only possess the nature of Christ Jesus, because my old sin nature *died* at the moment of salvation. I later physically acted out this salvation truth at my Water Baptism, by going down under the water. (Even though, the death of my sin nature had been earlier explained to me by my Pastor, I obviously hadn't fully understood the true significance of it, until quite recently.)

On the Cross, Jesus Christ broke the "power" of sin: *"For sin shall not have dominion over you, for you are not under law but under grace." Romans 6:14.* However, if you seriously believe you are still under law, then sin will keep on having dominion over you.

Before salvation, we sinned out of habit, because our thought pattern was ignorant of God's Word. To renew our mind, we need to feed on the *"incorruptible seed of God's Word"* and keep on planting it in the garden of our heart. Know that whatever is growing in our "inner garden" is what we've planted, or what we've allowed others to plant there.

This is true with a natural physical garden and it is also true spiritually in our life. The purpose of all seed planting is to produce a particular harvest. Therefore, a Christian's outward behavior begins on the inside, according to the knowledge of God's Word that has been planted there. The more knowledge that we have of God's Word, the more we will reflect His nature outwardly to others.

A definition of insanity would be to repeatedly do the "same" thing, but expecting different outcomes. Therefore, we will not be able to renew our mind, unless we both read and meditate on what God says. Meditation is focusing on something to the point, that it doesn't leave our consciousness. Satan's twisted form of meditation produces worry and loss of inner peace, but God's form of meditation results in liberating freedom in our soul area.

At salvation, we became a brand new creation: *"Therefore, if anyone is in Christ, he is a new creation, old things have passed away; behold all things have become new." 2 Corinthians 5:17.* This is present tense truth for every born-again believer. You are not the person you once were, because you no longer are part of Satan's kingdom, you are in God's kingdom.

At salvation, we come under the empowerment of God's grace instead of being under Satan's control. We need to fully understand His grace and what it has accomplished in our life. For example: when Jesus rose from the dead, He defeated Satan's dominion over us. We are no longer slaves to a brutal taskmaster, because we belong to Christ: *"Therefore you are no longer a slave but a son, and if a son, then an heir of God through Christ."* *Galatians 4:7*

Although we are on earth physically, we are living in a new dimension spiritually; we have been legally adopted and we now rightfully belong to the royal family of God. As family members, we have a royal inheritance to legally claim and to act upon. Just like the early Apostle, the prison door has been opened and we have been set free by the grace of God.

While-ever we are in our physical body, we need to know that repentance and confession of sin go hand in hand. (1 John 1:9) Repentance is a deep desire to change our ways because we know that whenever we sin, we grieve the heart of God. Godly sorrow on our part will deliver us whenever we slip into sin's grip.

"He who covers his sins will not prosper, but whoever confesses and forsakes them will have mercy." Proverbs 28:13. By repentance, we receive God's mercy. There is a big difference between grace and mercy. "Grace" is when we receive something good that we don't deserve, like salvation. "Mercy," on the other hand, is when we don't receive what we do truly deserve, like punishment for a particular sin.

For example: Jesus uniquely displayed both mercy and grace toward the woman caught in the act of adultery in John 8:3-11. By the legal requirement of the Law, Jesus had power to condemn her. Instead, He chose to extend mercy to her; therefore, she didn't receive what she legally deserved. Jesus then said to the woman: *"Go and sin no more."* In this, He conveyed His grace to her, as no word of God is void of power, according to Isaiah 55:11

His amazing words gave her the ability to overcome in this area. (Luke 1:37- with God nothing is impossible.) Mercy spared her the judgment of the Law and grace gave her undeserved, overcoming power to resist future temptation.

I want to now speak to those who want to go deeper in their walk with the Holy Spirit.

In Chapter 47, The Prophet Ezekiel speaks about a river that brings healing and an abundance of all things good. Some believers come to this river and put their feet in and then back away. Some of them follow Jesus to a point where it's comfortable and they are happy to play in the shallows. Others go right out into the water of the Holy Spirit right up to their head, but with their feet still on the ground. But God's Word encourages us to push further to a point where you can't reach the ground. This is the point where you are not in control anymore, for you have totally surrendered yourself to the desires of the Holy Spirit.

Some of my readers will be in the shallows now. They have been used by God often and they enjoy a measure of His presence, but they are hungry for more. To these people, I ask you to simply pray to the Lord and ask Him to lead you further into the water. The Lord is faithful, but the Holy Spirit and the Lord are gentlemen, they will not move you deeper until you really want to go deeper and you are ready for it.

For those of you who are up to your head in the river, you are having a great life. It can be quite scary to be so deep and you can be a little fearful of actually letting go of control of your life. But you already know that Jesus and the Holy Spirit have so much more enjoyment and adventure for you. When you let go, you soon will discover that you still have the choice to follow the leadings of the Holy Spirit in every action, but at this stage, you will be so in love with Jesus and the experience, that you will never want to resist anymore.

Living over your head in the river should be the goal of every Christian. It is such a delight and it's such a joyful place to be. In the river, there is peace and joy everlasting. When you live over your head in the river of God, you are immersed in the Holy Spirit.

It actually doesn't really matter if you are not loved or understood by everyone. Jesus certainly wasn't. You may even be considered weird and become like an outcast to people. You may find that much conversation, even by Christians, is shallow and has no depth to it. Instead, you will become hungry and thirsty to be fed and to drink from Heaven. When you live in the river, many books won't hold your attention for long. Even promising books with good reviews and good blurbs will be left unread after a couple of chapters. You will learn to commune with God and His Son and the Holy Spirit. You will learn to let Them speak to you and ponder Their wisdom and live and act in that wisdom.

When you let go and you live in the river, you won't need to go to the latest conference to be taught. You won't need someone to pray for you to receive an impartation. You will have God imparting to you wisdom and fresh manna each day. You will have impartations coming direct from the Throne-Room and coming upon you sometimes without you even knowing. You may have a particular mantle come upon you sometimes without your knowledge.

You will have "purpose" show itself to you and you will just swim in ecstasy and things that are considered to be profound to others will just come into your spirit. When you swim in the river and you live in the river all the time, you will walk in the Spirit all the time. It will no longer be a conscious choice to follow the leadings of the Holy Spirit like it once was, you will simply live and breathe and God will possess you and you will just be One with Him.

This is the oneness that Jesus prayed for His disciples, then and in the future: He prayed: *"I do not pray for these alone, but also for those who will believe in Me through their word; that they all may be one, as You, Father, are in Me, and I in You; that they also may be one in Us, that the world may believe that You sent Me.*

And the glory which You gave Me I have given them, that they may be one just as We are one." John 17:20-22.

From this Oneness, you will no longer have to think what the Lord wants you to do each day, you will simply get up and start to do it naturally. You will finish one thing and then you will be led into something else. When you are living in the river, you will discover that you are in a place of eternal rest. To those who are stuck in sin, I want to offer you "hope" to be free of sin. If you're just paddling or up to your head in the river, I want to give you the assurance that "in Christ," you can succeed in whatever field of endeavor God has for you.

I love my life now because I know that I am living with eternity in mind. I feel that I am enjoying my cake and having it stored up at the same time. I boast only in God's extravagant love that he offers to every one of His family members. I encourage you to come into the river of God. I know that you can experience all that I am experiencing because I can testify to its reality.

Even in saying this, I still have really sad days when the devil puts depression onto me and I become drained of all my human strength and have to call out for help just to do simple mundane things. At those times, I just need to concentrate on just getting my feet wet again and coming in and out of the river. I remember going out into the deep and being afraid to go past where my feet could touch the ground. I remember the fear of not ever being in control again. And then I remember just letting go and being lost in the river.

Write to me at survivors.sanctuary@gmail.com if you are up to your head and you want me to personally pray for you. For all others, I offer this prayer:

Heavenly Father, Teach Your people to walk in the Spirit. Cause them to conquer personal sin and then lead them to walk in obedience to Your good and perfect will. Lead them into a lifestyle of obedience so that it becomes instinctive to them.

Lead them into Your River and encourage them to go right out into the deep water and give them the boldness to let go and step right out where their feet cannot touch the ground. Be with them, prosper them and give them Your awesome favor throughout their whole life. I ask this in the precious Name of Jesus. Amen.

CHAPTER 14
DAY TO DAY LIFE IN THE KINGDOM

Everyone on earth has been *uniquely* created by God. Some people may have a physical double in the world somewhere, but no one else will have my unique soul. Therefore, what God has individually called me to do is not necessarily exactly what He has in mind for you.

Christians share a common calling: to be Christ to others and to tell people about Heaven's perfect love story. (Matthew 28:19-30) How we go about that will depend on the spiritual understanding that we have of God's Word and the abilities and opportunities God has blessed us with. Part of me is really excited because I know in my spirit that all Christians who can hear Jesus speak as clearly as I can could very easily prophesy like I do.

A general definition of prophecy would be: "telling forth God's truth and will." I would dearly love to see every Christian I know to begin to prophesy and I guess if I was a gifted healer, I would love to encourage everyone to seek healing as well.

The entire Bible is a product of the Holy Spirit, who is not only "the Spirit of truth" – see John 16:13, but in Revelation 19:10, He is called the "Spirit of prophecy." When you are gifted in the prophetic, the Holy Spirit uses you to speak out a personal prophecy that will encourage and edify another person. The fact of the matter is that you are you. I say this because even though you can develop and mature, you can't change *anything about you unless you personally want to make that change.* I pray that this book has said enough to encourage you to go on and do more in God's Kingdom.

Jesus delights in helping those who want to be helped and yet sometimes, we might really want help from Him and He seems not to answer. This can be difficult to deal with. I believe that there are many people who can easily walk in the supernatural, and though others really want to walk in it, they seem not to be able to. This can bring confusion to them and others. My advice would be to go on praying that God will reveal His personal purpose for your life.

Walking hand in hand with Jesus is an exciting way to live. Having your everyday directions coming from the Holy Spirit is very reassuring. We know from the Scriptures that the early disciples after Pentecost walked very close to Jesus. When we have a good idea as to what we are here to do, life becomes much easier. However, everyone's life still has personal challenges to overcome, regardless of their particular calling.

"These things I have spoken to you, that in Me you may have peace. In the world you will have tribulation; but be of good cheer, I have overcome the world." John 16:33.

Here, Jesus told us to expect tribulation in the world. The Greek word for tribulation is "thlipsis" and this word is used for crushing grapes or olives in a press. This is not the experience that one would willingly choose, but if the perfect Son of God suffered so much opposition and tribulation on earth, so too, will we.

The Apostle, Paul, was privileged by God to write most of the New Testament Epistles, yet he suffered tremendously. You see a list of his sufferings in 2 Corinthians 11:23-27. We complain of a slight headache or a rebuke by someone, yet this very learned and humble man, who had suffered so much for his faith, wanted above all else to magnify the Lordship of Jesus Christ. He said: *"For to me, to live is Christ, and to die is gain." Philippians 2:20* Then later, he shared his heart's motivation: *"that I may know Him and the power of His resurrection, and the fellowship of His sufferings, being conformed to His death." Philippians 3:10*

My Bible notes say that: "to know Jesus was Paul's primary pursuit in life. After his recent past as a persecutor of Christians and through his "superior" religious activities as a Pharisee, Paul came to the liberating conclusion that all was rubbish compared to knowing the Lord. Paul was a lover of God and as such, He was never a user of God. And whether he moved in Christ's resurrection power, or was stretched to his last ounce of endurance, it mattered little. For Paul, it was all a part of the most fulfilling journey of all; truly knowing God. With an attitude like that, we can see why God chose to use Paul to pen His words to us.

Andrew Wommack, in his book called "Effortless Change," teaches us how to have victory in the storms of life. In his book, he said that one day, Jesus taught on ten parables, pointing out that God's words are like "seed" in our life. Jesus knew exactly what was about to come against His disciples in their boat, so he decided to test their listening retention. As they approached their small fishing boat, He casually gave a new "seed" to them by saying: *"Let's pass over unto the other side."* (Mark 4:35) He then rested in the bottom of the boat.

A savage storm suddenly developed, causing the waves to flood the boat. Jesus remained at rest for He wanted to test His disciple's reactions. In fear of their lives, the terrified men woke Him up and accused Him of not caring about them. (Mark 4:38) That's so typical of us - we hear bad news and all of a sudden we panic. We say: "Where were you Lord?" We basically place blame for negative things onto God as if it's His fault.

Not every problem we have is God ordained: He didn't order the storm. The desperate disciples wanted Jesus to start doing His share of work and bail out the water. They were angry that He was sleeping while they were about to die. But, you see, Jesus had already done His part because He had given His disciples a word or "seed" which was: *"Let us pass over unto the other side."* By faith, they could have released the life in His word and commanded the elements to be still in the power of Jesus' Name. Their fear ruled their hearts and not the Word of God. How would we react in the same situation?

Jesus has given us all His words to claim, yet instead of claiming what is rightfully ours, we approach the Lord like a beggar and not like the legally adopted heirs that we are. By using God's life-filled Words, we can change negative situations in our life. We are told in 2 Peter 1:3 that *"His divine power has given to us all things that pertain to life and godliness, through the knowledge of Him who called us by glory and virtue."*

When we boldly claim God's Word, the "power" in His Word will begin to release the "life" in it, because God's Seed is incorruptible and unchanging. We have God's assurance on this, He said: *"so shall My word be that goes forth from My mouth; It shall not return to Me void, But it shall accomplish what I please and it shall prosper in the thing for which I sent it."* Isaiah 55:10-11.

By allowing their emotions to rule, the disciples failed the test and most of us would probably do the same thing. Jesus then rebuked the wind and storm: He then spoke "peace" to the sea and turned to His pupils and said: *"Why are you so fearful? How is it that you have no faith?"* (*Mark 4:40*) He was angry at their unbelief for He had spent so much time explaining to them that the seed of God's Word contains power and life. They had even received private insight from Him when the crowd had gone. (Mark 4:34)

They should have taken their God-given authority and rebuked the wind, the storm and the sea in the Name of Jesus! As their Teacher, He was sowing Himself into them, so that they could do His work when He was not around.

Christians are asking God to do what He told "them" to do, so they are not being obedient to His Words. Jesus told us to advance His Kingdom on earth; He told us to heal the sick and be His ambassadors. Jesus taught that "life" is in His Seed, but we aren't planting His Seed into our heart and meditating on it, so that it will bear fruit. God isn't asleep; we are the ones who are sleeping. We are asking Him to do things that we should do ourselves.

The key to victory is to exercise, by faith, our spiritual authority in Christ and then enter into His rest. Until we go to glory, we will constantly have challenges because we live in a world controlled by the devil. Originally, God gave Adam the authority to rule on earth, but he lost that authority when he didn't stand up to the devil. Adam's mistake was heeding Eve's voice, rather than the voice of God. She had been genuinely deceived by the devil, but Adam should have exercised authority over the devil and stopped her from eating the forbidden fruit.

Although He is not the source of tribulation, God will use trials to re-shape us into being the person He wants us to be. At great cost, God has graciously given all of us a "free-will" but we only have power to rule our own will, not the will of anyone else. Instead, we are to pray about our problems regarding other people.

There are many other problems in life that God expects us to handle simply by using the authority He has given to us. Instead of begging God to solve these problems, we have been told to speak directly to the problem itself, in the power of Jesus' Name.

Later on in the Book of Mark, the astonished disciples saw the withered fig tree that their Master had cursed and Jesus said to them: *"For assuredly I say to you, whoever says to this mountain, 'Be removed and be cast into the sea,' and does not doubt in his heart, but believes that those things he says will be done, he will have whatever he says." Mark 11:23*

How do we put this into practice? If we have a headache, or the symptoms of a cold, or whatever; instead of taking our problem to God, use the authority we have been given. Don't pray about it, but speak directly to the headache and command it to go in Jesus' Name. All sickness and pain is the work of the enemy and it has no place in our life. We have been given the authority to do this and the story about the storm re-affirms our authority.

Reading stories about people who have experienced great success will inspire us to move toward success ourselves. Some people's amazing impact in the spiritual domain leaves a legacy long after they have been upgraded to Heaven. It is certainly my hope that both I and my readers can make a positive, lasting impact in the lives of others. If we shine the light of Jesus well enough, we may, like Joseph and many other Old and New Testament saints, become a light on a hill for our generation. To do this, we are to take aboard God's Word and be obedient to it in the grace power of the Holy Spirit in us.

Let me challenge you, how can "the way you live today" best impact your area of influence and also cause you to lay up treasure for your life in Heaven? To my mind, "living with eternity in mind" is the way we are meant to live as it will change our outlook about almost everything. Unbelievers mostly think only of themselves but let us do better. I pray that all my readers will see the impact that they could make if they thought beyond themselves and lived a day to day life that represents Christ to those who know Him not.

My Testimony: Soon after my marriage breakdown and on-ongoing custody battle where I failed to get joint custody of my young son, I came under so much stress that I had a nervous breakdown. Because of the nature of the stress, I came out the other side of that breakdown with a mental illness that changed my whole life. However, it didn't take God by surprise.

Over the years, I have learnt how to rest in His love. He and I have a good relationship, which may not have been true if life had been easy for me. Even though I have struggled for over twenty years, God has never left me to cope by myself. Medication helps me to have a life that is fairly balanced and it also keeps me out of hospital, yet the irregular periods of depression drain me quite often.

Despite my illness, I have learnt how to prophesy and have ministered to many thousands of people, encouraging them in a unique way. I have also been inspired to write hundreds of articles and a number of books. Paul speaks about us glorying in our weaknesses. I am so thankful for the Lord Jesus that He uses me despite my illness. It thrills my heart that the Lord has given me the ability to reach other people through the gifts that He has given me.

So much of my character has been carved out through this mental illness and though I know that sickness and disease both come from Satan, I feel that I am a far more patient and well-rounded Christian guy because for my struggles. In this respect, I hope that one day, in a small way, I can identify with Joseph in the Bible.

My Bible notes say that "the life of Joseph displayed God's sovereign ability to bring to pass His destiny for an obedient believer." Joseph, as a young lad, received a vision of God's plan for his life which had angered his brothers. But later, it seemed that this vision had died and that his life would be wasted away in slavery and prison. Nevertheless, Joseph remained faithful to God.

Joseph held no resentment or un-forgiveness towards his brothers because he saw God in his life. Years later, when his brothers came to seek his forgiveness, his reply to them was: "God sent me before you to preserve prosperity for you in the earth, and to save your lives by a great deliverance. So now, it was not you who sent me here, but God." Genesis 47:5-6a.

Later on, when his brothers wanted to be his servants, Joseph humbly responded: "But as for you, you meant evil against me, but God meant it for good."Genesis 50:20. Yes, things happen in life that may seem unfair or even frightening, but when we know emphatically that God is a good God – always, then we can place our faith in the power of His Word so that negative situations can actually change into something good.

For example: I am just one of millions of people who struggle with sickness in the world. I know that my story and my illness can actually encourage other people to press on and to feel better. If you are suffering, I pray that you also will be comforted. My advice is to trust in God's sovereign providence. He causes all things to work for your good as you remain faithful to His calling and purpose for you. We have God promise on this in Romans 8:28.

CHAPTER 15
THE "SUPERNATURAL" LIFE

There are many Christians who live supernatural lives and the Apostle Paul certainly did. We know through his writings that he healed people and he even raised a dead man who had gone to sleep during a meeting and had fallen out of a window. Paul also saw Jesus in visions, and he went to Heaven at least once whether in a vision or in the body; he could not ascertain which, so vivid was the experience.

Salvation is the greatest miracle of all, but Paul's salvation had been even more miraculous than most others. As a highly trained orthodox Jew, he had been an extremely zealous Pharisee who was on a particular mission one day to arrest some Christians. However, unbeknown to him, he had actually been persecuting the long awaited Jewish Messiah!

We read in *Acts 9:3-4* *"As he journeyed he came near Damascus and suddenly a light shone around him from Heaven. Then he fell to the ground, and heard a voice saying to him "Saul, Saul, why are you persecuting Me?"* Jesus Christ Himself appeared to Saul and converted him on the spot and later, Jesus renamed him Paul.

Because Jesus knew this man's intense zeal for the things of God, he was mightily used by God to strengthen the New Testament believers both then and in the future. One of the many personal revelations that Paul received from the Holy Spirit was the positive affirmation that: *"I can do all things through Christ who strengthens me." Philippians 4:13*

We too, therefore, can be confident that when God wants us to do something, He is able to supply the strength and the ability to do it. I have spoken on this verse previously but it is one that I depend on often, so it is a favorite of mine. In context, Jesus had been telling His disciples that it was very difficult for a rich person to be saved. *"When His disciples heard it, they were greatly astonished, saying, 'Who then can be saved?' Jesus replied, "With men this is impossible, but with God all things are possible." Matthew 19:25-26.*

There is nothing wrong about being rich, but money can be like a god in some people's life. Worldly pleasures can blind a person to their own spiritual poverty. In contrast, the spiritually rich care little for the temporary attractions that the world has to offer.

After the miracle of personal salvation, moving in the gifts of the Holy Spirit is another aspect of living the supernatural life. We are to realize that the Holy Spirit is just as active today as He was in the Book of Acts. Some people struggle to heal for quite a while and then they seem to catch on to the gift and go on to heal hundreds of people. One person who comes to mind is Roger Sapp. He says that many people have a revelation of Jesus as Savior but they don't yet have the revelation of Jesus as the Divine Healer.

We readily believe that Jesus can forgive our sins and His Holy Spirit can cleanse and keep us, but many Christians still doubt that healing was also purchased for us at the cross, by the blood of Jesus.

The original New Testament was written in the Greek language. My Bible tells me "the different meanings of the Greek word "sozo" can be used for save; heal; cure; preserve; keep safe and sound; recue from danger or destruction; and deliver. Sozo saves from physical death by healing and from spiritual death by forgiving sin and its effect. Sozo, in primitive cultures, is translated simply, "to give new life" and "to cause to have a new heart." A great book on this subject is called "Healing the Sick" by T.L.

Osborn – it's not only about God wanting us well, but it's also about having faith in the absolute goodness of God.

As I have said before, God has given me the ability to be able to move in the three gifts of the Holy Spirit used in prophecy. I can move in word of knowledge, word of wisdom, and prophecy. The gifts of prophecy are wonderful to walk in, because others can be really blessed by a prophetic anointing in your life. Having the ability to tell a total stranger about a part of their life and give them direction from God is a wonderful gift. Many people are learning to prophesy these days. Prophecy is not only fairly easy to do, but it is very beneficial to the body of Christ.

Meeting Jesus in visions is very exciting for me. Jesus is an awesome friend and when people are open, He can come and visit them. I have many good memories of Jesus coming to see me. Jesus has even brought with Him other saints for me to meet from Heaven. I have been fortunate to have quite a number of conversations with Jesus face to face. Jesus loves to visit His people and sometimes, reading books that are written about others meeting Jesus will give you a special impartation.

It is also possible to meet Jesus in the flesh. I have been very blessed to meet Jesus in the flesh more than once. When He comes in the flesh, He might not at first identify Himself, but may leave it up to your own spirit to recognize Him and interact with Him, if you have the courage. One time, I saw Jesus in the flesh and I talked to Him for about ten minutes where he shared what he meant in the Gospels. This was a truly memorable experience. At the end of that encounter, He disappeared into thin air just to show me that the encounter was Divine.

I actually believe that it's part of our new kingdom birthright as a Christian to visit Heaven in visions. Scripture teaches that we are seated in Heavenly places. By being seated in Heaven, surely we need only to look around and marvel at its perfection. I have certainly enjoyed what I have seen. Not only have I visited my future mansion and children up there, but I have been to the Throne Room and other places in Heaven. Knowing my eternal home and seeing it gives me a greater love for the unsaved and doing things God's way.

We also have the ability to meet angels and communicate with them. Some angels do not have permission to speak with us, but many times, they can speak to us and encourage us. Angels are with us all the time and certain angels can come with special ministry gifts that God wants us to move in. Some believers have been known to have a healing angel travel with them in their ministry. I have an angel that, at times, has helped me prophecy. Sometimes I have had an angel come down with a scroll, and on it was a prophecy for a person that was dictated to me. Angels are fun-loving and they enjoy helping us with our life on earth.

The writer of Hebrews says about angels: *"Are they not all ministering spirits sent forth to minister for those who will inherit salvation."* Hebrews 1:14.

The note in my Bible says: "A careful study will reveal that the New Testament activity of angels usually revolves around the ministry of Jesus and the establishment of His church on earth. They are ministering spirits, or Heavenly assistants, who are continually active today in building the body of Christ – advancing the ministry of Jesus and the building of His church."

There are many books on the supernatural and some of them have impartations in them. I read a book called *"Face to Face Appearances from Jesus"* by David Taylor and after reading that book, I had more visions of Jesus. Part of the power of testimony is that it increases our faith and that faith allows us to experience more of the things of God.

God would prefer all His people to live supernatural lives. Moses, in the Old Testament, wrote in Numbers 11:29 that he wished all men could be prophets. I think many people are held back because they don't hear of ordinary people doing

127

extraordinary things. Paul, in the New Testament, said in 1 Corinthians 14:5 that he wished that all could prophesy. I want to encourage you that I am just an ordinary guy. There is nothing special about me. I have just done what I have felt led to do by God each day. Some people look at my supernatural experiences and wish they too could have them. I feel that God would love everyone to draw closer to Him and let them share in what I have seen.

CHAPTER 16
HELPING OTHERS SEE JESUS

There have been numerous people who have casually read parts of the New Testament Bible that has been purposely left in a drawer in a hotel or motel by the Gideon's Association. As a result, salvations have occurred. However, most people come to the Lord through a church service or by the personal witness of a believer. We may not be consciously aware of it, but people are always watching us and making judgments on how we carry out our daily affairs.

These people may be seeking God and are observing us to see if our walk is authentic and whether the Christian life is somewhat better than what they already have. Therefore, it's very important that we should be seen as "salt" to those we come in contact with. Jesus said:

"You are the salt of the earth; but if the salt loses its flavour, how shall it be seasoned? It is then good for nothing but to be thrown out and trampled underfoot by men." Matthew 5:13

Salt has long been used as a natural preserver of food. It doesn't stop meat from eventually going off, but it considerably slows down the process. As salt, we are meant to give the world some stability and a way of seeing what is right. The world's morals are rapidly decaying; they are in fact going down such a slippery slope that maybe one day, there will be no rules whatsoever.

We have been warned of this. *"For men will be lovers of themselves, lovers of money, boasters, proud, blasphemers, disobedient to parents, unthankful, unholy, unloving, unforgiving, slanderers, without self-control, brutal, despisers of good, traitors, headstrong, haughty, loves of pleasure rather than lovers of God.* 2 Timothy 3:2-4

As believers, we need to resist being part of this terrible downward trend. In doing so, we will be reminding others of what is right and what Godly standards are. Our actions and attitudes are to be a voice of reason, silently declaring to our friends what God requires. We don't need to be pushy, but when friends ask advice, we should be able to help them in a godly way.

At least two times, Paul has urged us to: *"Walk in wisdom toward those who are outside, redeeming the time. Let your speech always be with grace, seasoned with salt, that you may know how you ought to answer each one."* Colossians 4:5-6. See also Ephesians 4:26

The word "circumspectly" in Ephesians 4:26, means to walk cautiously, sensitively, as a person would walk through thorny terrain. The phrase "redeeming the time" is capitalizing on every appropriate opportunity. Therefore, we are to sensitively take advantage of opportunities to be both salt and light to those we come into contact with.

Salt not only helps to preserve food, but it also brings out the flavor in other foods. Therefore, life on earth should be more exciting and more fulfilling with Christians in it. We should definitely not be people who are known for nagging or complaining. Instead, we should be known as people who are motivated by high standards and who constantly demonstrate love towards others. God wants His people to walk in wisdom and to reflect the love and grace of Christ in our speech and actions.

We are to enjoy our life, but we are not to allow the negative standards of the world to become our standards. We are to be seen as different, but not weird! We should not be so spiritual that unbelievers can't relate to us, yet we should put Jesus first in our life in all matters and treat people how He would treat them.

We are to particularly walk in wisdom when it comes to people who are not yet saved. It would probably not be wise to share our Heavenly visions with them, but we might share about the healing that happened at church. Some unbelievers already think that Christians are weird, so it's best not to give a reason that will add strength to their suspicions.

Unbelievers particularly need to receive love and grace from us. In fact, some may even treat us unkindly to test whether our faith is genuine or whether we are just 'Christians' in name only. People who are seeking God will also ask us difficult questions. We need to exercise grace and wisdom when we give our opinion, as sometimes, it's not the answer to the question, but our attitude towards it that the person is really interested in. In Paul's letters to the New Testament churches, He always prayed that believers would have the grace of God.

We are to try to keep a cool head as sometimes, a person will deliberately bait us, just to see if we become flustered. We may not be aware of this when they start to question us, so keeping a cool head like Paul suggests is a good mindset to have. If you feel that you are getting irritated, it's best to stop the conversation and promise them that you will discuss it another day. If people ask us a question that we have no answer for, just tell them that you will have to do some research, or tell them you will need to ask your Pastor for his opinion on the matter.

The important thing is that we need to stand out as being "positively" different to those who know not God. Our motives, our speech, and our behavior should be unashamedly different to that of unbelievers. However, many Christians feel the need to be loved and accepted so strongly that they are easily intimidated. Therefore, their speech is no different to others in the world. These Christians really need to receive the "liberating revelation" of God's amazing grace demonstrated on the cross for them personally.

People really need to see for themselves the hope and the peace that we have in Christ as everyone, deep-down, longs for these two attributes. Paul gave us a splendid recipe to develop an honorable thought life, which the grace of Jesus produces. He said: *"Finally, brethren, whatever things are true, whatever things are noble, whatever things are just, whatever things are pure, whatever things are lovely, whatever things are of good report, if there is any virtue and if there is anything praiseworthy - meditate on these things." Philippians 4:8*

Too often, Christians revert to carnal thinking and are quick to criticize others, or to make harsh judgements about people or situations. These believers will verbalize their negative opinions and so they react just like the people of the world. If we train our thought life like Paul suggests in the above verse, then our tongue will not be so quick to condemn others.

An Old Testament equivalent says: *"Pleasant words are like a honeycomb, sweetness to the soul and health to the bones." Proverbs 16:24.* Wouldn't the Christian experience be different if we spoke and acted this way more often? Our body would be healthier as well.

The world's daily news headlines are mostly filled with increasingly bad reports, but most people really enjoy hearing uplifting stories that cause them to smile. It would be wonderful to be known as a person who brings joy to a workplace and who never gossips or pull others down. People would be able to share their burdens with someone like that and may, over time, even take aboard some of the truths of God's Word.

Isaiah 55:11 gives us the confident assurance that His incorruptible Word will not return to Him void, but it will accomplish its purpose. Pray for opportunities to sow Truth Seed into people. *"The word of God is quick* (alive) *and powerful, and sharper than any two edged sword." Hebrews 4:12.* When we plant natural seed, it can already be corrupted: it can be tainted or rotten with no life in it, but God's Seed is totally incorruptible. (1 Peter 1:23)

Most people, before they are saved, have already met a Christian whom they have admired and respected. When they are faced with the decision to give their life to the Lord, God will remind them of those who have impacted their life and that person could be you. You could be a bright shining light to all of your friends and be there for any of them if they want to talk to you. You can be that safe person who they can confidently share their heart with and open up to, when life gets too tough for them. It's so important to know the Word of God, so that the Holy Spirit can retrieve it from our memory, when we need to pass it on to others.

Everyone needs someone whom they can share their deep concerns with. Sharing your own particular struggles and desires often opens the door for others to do likewise. Unbelievers need to know that you understand them and are not in any way judging them. Being a loyal friend in this way is actually helping someone see Jesus.

When you are mindful of God's presence and you pray for your friends to be saved, they have a good chance of experiencing salvation one day. Who knows, your friend may desire to be like you and they might even ask you about your faith and you can lead them to the Lord. Paul said: *"Let your gentleness be known to all men. The Lord is at hand." Philippians 4:5*

I am a gentle person who is loving and emotional majority of the time. Paul encourages us to be gentle with people. Being gentle with others is a way of treating them in such a way that is infused with love and grace. You will note that Paul says "all" people here. He doesn't say, be gentle to people who are gentle to you. Their treatment toward you should not dictate your treatment of them, because that's the way of the world and we are to be different.

An excellent way to help people see Jesus in you is to show genuine love to those who rarely receive it. These people may be rather rough looking and their speech may be somewhat colorful, but they are often easier to minister love to than anyone else. Sure, they will initially suspect that you want to take advantage of them, but when they see that you genuinely want to befriend them, things can go well.

I know this to be true, because I serve coffee to homeless people twice a week. Some of my customers have learnt to be suspicious of anyone who bothers to talk to them, but they enjoy a free coffee and will chat with me, after a while. Always bear in mind that all people are worthy of love. When you live a life that helps people see Jesus, you are living for eternity.

———————————

CHAPTER 17
MY THOUGHTS ON GIVING

I feel that the Apostle Paul said it so well when he said: *"Command those who are rich in this present age not to be haughty, nor to trust in uncertain riches but in the living God, who gives us richly all things to enjoy. Let them do good, that they be rich in good works, ready to give, willing to share, storing up for themselves a good foundation for the time to come, that they may lay hold on eternal life." 1Timothy 6:17-19*

Many people might read these verses and excuse themselves by saying, "I'm not rich!" But most of us in the West are indeed rich, compared to people in the rest of the world. I am on a disability pension and even my income is way above most people's income in the world.

God wants all believers to be rich in good works, so it's very important for us to be a good witness to the goodness of God to all the people that we do life with. As I have said before, there are many easy and yet good things that we can do. We can say 'Hello' and 'goodbye' to a bus driver. We can be cordial to shop keepers and be kind to people who serve us in restaurants. We can be God's light and shine out as pleasantly different to others in the world.

There are many ways that we can shine in this indifferent world of ours. Being sensitive to the Holy Spirit will allow us to find new ways to stand out as being different in a pleasant and casual way. Another way to shine is to be sensitive to people's financial needs. Being ready to give to others comes down to an attitude of mind. If we are not prepared to give, no amount of people begging us to do so will change our attitude. But if we have a healthy attitude when it comes to giving, the Holy Spirit will use us to help others in need.

God has gifted me with the "Gift of Giving" so I just love to give and I wish all people were gifted in this way. Giving to others is an enjoyable lifestyle and it doesn't take long to make it a habit. Once giving is habitual, you will enjoy it and you will bless so many other people.

Some people really need others to share with them. It's as easy as going out for lunch or dinner after church and noticing that someone has not ordered anything. These people are probably hungry, but they may have to budget carefully. However, they don't allow their financial embarrassment to stop them from joining in a time of Christian fellowship. We can quietly and politely tell this person that we want to buy them something and that they don't need to pay us back. When you are open to sharing with others, God can really use you.

By being Christ-like to others we, like the Apostle Paul, can personally discover that *"God shall supply all our need according to His riches in glory by Christ Jesus." Philippians 4:19.* Also, by taking the opportunity of happily giving and sharing, believers are building up a good foundation for their future in eternity.

Personally, I am very aware that God knows my every need. Just this week, I was out of money and someone placed a very timely donation into my 'Paypal' account. The money was just enough for me to get through the week. God is aware of your needs as well. He may not supply money for our lusts, but He can and will supply money for our genuine needs.

God is a good God – all the time. Really knowing this increases our faith in His goodness. He loves us and delights in working through us, to others. I find that when I give to worthy causes, it fills my life with a wider outlook then just having a narrow focus in life. Giving to others not only brings joy to me, but it demonstrates the love of God to the person I give to.

When you have revelation that you are just a *"steward of the Lord's money,"* then you will be much better at using it for God's glory. But if you consider that you have earned your money and you can spend it anyway you want to, then it can be very difficult to use it to bless others. I want you to know that living a life where you are continually blessing other people with the Lord's money can be an extremely rewarding life.

There are countless worthy organizations, both secular and Christian, that people can financially support. Some organizations list particular things you can contribute to, within their organization. Personally, I contribute to Christian ministries and I prefer to know where my donation is being used, rather than it being gobbled up in massive administration costs. Yet, I realize that these costs are necessary. Whenever the Lord places a particular need in my heart, He gives me the joy of contributing to that specific need.

The Parable of the Talents and the Parable of the Minas speak of a person who failed to invest what the Master had given to them. In both instances, the Master was quite angry with the person who had not received a return on His money. These parables should be a sobering warning to us. God uses the money He has blessed us with to test our love for Him. Life is not just about us, God wants to use us to bless others and this very often includes blessing others financially.

Andrew Wommack, in his book, "Financial Stewardship" says that there are two dominant heart conditions when it comes to money: "eaters" and "sowers." Eaters only give their left-over money to God, while sowers seek His kingdom first. This is the kind of believer God is searching for. The reason that God wants His children to give is so that others can be blessed. That's not all, in the process, God just delights to bless a cheerful giver.

For the Christian, tithing isn't mandatory as it was in the Old Testament days. Christians give out of genuine appreciation for all that God did for them through the sacrificial death and victorious resurrection of Christ Jesus. Therefore, Christians give so that other people may discover for themselves the goodness of God.

A truth that I personally delight in, is that God is the true source of every good thing: *"Every good gift and every perfect gift is from above, and comes down from the Father of lights, with whom there is no variation or shadow of turning. Of His own will He brought us forth by the word of truth, that we might be a kind of firstfruits of His creatures." James 1:17-18.*

The "word of truth" is, of course, Jesus, who provided the gift of regeneration to all who ask for it. A Christian, therefore, is to see everything they have as belonging to God. He wants us to be wise stewards of any money that He has provided for us. We may believe that we have provided our money by working for it. However, we must recognize that all the "abilities" we have and every favorable "opportunity" to work has actually come from God.

God wants us to treat money like seed to be sown. If we consume every dollar that comes our way, we aren't investing in our future. Tithing is the smart thing for every Christian to do. It's not God's fault if we eat-up all our seed! We need to be disciplined enough to take a portion of what God has given us and sow it into our future by placing our money into God's Heavenly bank. Earthly banks may let us down but God's Heavenly bank is as reliable and trustworthy as God Himself. Also, this bank pays very large dividends.

God loves us if we give ten percent, one percent or nothing. Tithing has nothing to do with how God relates to us, but tithing has a priceless benefit which many mature Christians can gladly testify to. If we truly see our finances as belonging to God, we will never have fear of financial stress, regardless of the world's worsening economy. When we listen to the television news about the economies of the world, we can be confident that God Himself is in charge of our wealth and He will see to it that we and our loved ones are cared for.

There is a huge difference between the Old and the New Testament principles. It's important to understand that God had to relate to His people differently before Christ, because God has said that natural man can't understand spiritual things. *"But the natural man does not receive the things of the Spirit of God, for they are foolishness to him; nor can he know them, because they are spiritually discerned." 1 Corinthians 2:14*

In the Old Testament, the Holy Spirit came "upon" a particular person for a certain time to do a specific job. Today, the Holy Spirit permanently indwells every single believer and gives them inner spiritual understanding. Because the Old Testament people lacked this kind of understanding, God had to apply discipline to them if they did the wrong thing, much the same as a parent will treat a young toddler. Until a child comes to the age of understanding, a parent will use suitable discipline to train them in safety matters and in other things.

We see in James 1:17 above that God has always been the same, it's just that He had to relate to His people differently before the cross of Jesus. Christians today are to tithe with a totally different motivation than people did under the Old Covenant.

I am aware that many of my readers may go to a prosperity-preaching church. In those churches week after week, the congregation hears a mini-sermon about the importance of giving financially. I certainly don't want to be another person giving such a sermon. But the fact remains that a Christian who sees their money as God's money, sees far more reward in their life than someone who has a tight hold on their wallet. I believe that our personal perception about money in this life will have eternal consequence.

For five days every ninety days, I can give my books away for free on Kindle. I say this not to boast, but as an example of

God blessing my heart motive for writing. This month, the total of my four books downloaded for free was over 2,000 copies. A person who is not an author cannot give that amount of books away in a month, but as an author, I can do this. It brings me so much joy knowing that so many lives can be affected in a good way by reading my books. What a wonderful way of spreading the good news of knowing Christ Jesus.

I have only spoken very briefly on this important subject, because I have grown up in a family that has a good understanding on the importance of giving. It has, therefore, never been a problem for me or my siblings to give to God and to others.

All the commandments that Jesus gave us are very wise including this one; He said: *"Do not lay up for yourselves treasures on earth, where moth and rust destroy and where thieves break in and steal; but lay up for yourselves treasures in Heaven, where neither moth nor rust destroys and where thieves do not break in and steal. For where your treasure is, there your heart will be also. Matthew 6:19-21*

I highly recommend Andrew Wommack's book called *Financial Stewardship.* Chapter Seven is particularly good; it covers the subject of tithing very well. You would be able to order it through most Christian book stores. Andrew has an extremely balanced view on subjects relating to the Christian life. Other books of his that are very helpful are "Effortless Change" (about the Word of God) and "A Better Way to Pray" and "The War is Over!" He is my favorite author and speaker, that's why I highly recommend his books and briefly summarize some of his teachings in my books. His powerful teaching on God's grace dramatically changed my whole Christian life.

CHAPTER 18
MAKING SATAN SQUIRM

Satan, our age-long enemy, hates all humans, but he especially hates the redeemed. He does his best to deceive us and to bring us into bondage and under his control. All mistruth and error essentially comes from him. We may not care to admit it, but all of us are susceptible to believe in some kind of error in our walk of faith. Satan is a professional liar, so his lies can be so convincing and plausible, that we may willingly take them aboard.

Satan loves to try and destroy us and all our relationships, particularly spiritual relationships. He wants to destroy our church, our hopes and our faith, so that we become ineffective in God's Kingdom. Satan wants to either steal or destroy everything that's good from everyone, not just believers. He certainly wants to steal the Christian's sense of worthiness and to keep them ignorant of their new identity in Christ. He tries to weigh believers down with guilt and condemnation, so as to steal their security and inner peace. Also, he whispers to unbelievers that they are hopeless sinners and God is not interested in them.

Jesus said of Satan: *"The thief does not come except to steal, and to kill, and to destroy. I have come that they may have life, and that they may have it more abundantly." John 10:10*

Believers must recognize that God has given them "His" peace based on the reconciliation work of the cross alone. *God's peace is actually a "covenant" peace because God is a covenant-keeping God.* At our salvation, His covenant peace came into our lives. Therefore, if ever we feel we have lost God's peace, we can know for sure that Satan has temporarily deceived us and is having a field day with us.

For example: within weeks of my mother's salvation, she met up with her cousin who was a fairly new Christian and had recently been deceived by a well known cult. My mother and her cousin spent hours discussing the Bible and that night, mum came home feeling that maybe she wasn't a Christian after all.

Thankfully, an elder in her church sensed in his spirit that something was wrong and said: "Okay June, what's happened, tell me all about it." That afternoon, he came to our home and for two hours, He patiently sat with her and dealt with the lies Satan had planted. Her comment was: "I never realized I had the peace of God, until I lost it! Now I understand His peace." She then sent a long letter to her cousin and she soon left the cult. I reckon Satan was really squirming when this godly elder was ministering to my mum.

The Lord led me to write a book called *"Your Identity in Christ."* You can read this small book in a few hours. Even though I say it myself, it's a good read. It's so vital that every Christian knows their true identity in Christ as it's the only way to successfully refute Satan's lies. It's actually a book I need to re-read myself. I say this because I continually have to remind myself of my position in Christ and all the salvation privileges that are mine to claim. Every believer is to be continually aware and absolutely confident of these spiritual truths, for they release ongoing power in a believer's life that really makes Satan squirm.

In Colossians 2:15, we read that Jesus, on the cross, once for all time, *disarmed principalities and powers, He made a public spectacle of them, triumphing over them in it."*

Paul reminds us of who we once were, he said: *"Even when we were* (spiritually) *dead in sin,* (God) *made us alive together with Christ (by grace you have been saved), and raised us up together, and made us sit together in the Heavenly places in Christ Jesus." Ephesians 2:5-6*

Paul says "we were dead" before salvation. Now, death is not like being sick - death means it's all over - as no one can be half dead or a little bit dead – the same as no woman can be a little bit pregnant. No, dead is dead! But at salvation, God supernaturally raised us up to be spiritually "alive" and seated us in Heavenly places in Christ.

Earlier, Paul had said that we had been objects of God's wrath, i.e. before faith, we were all once part of a corrupted and accursed mass that God had condemned. But through personal belief in Christ, God make spiritually "dead" people to come alive and He welcomes them into His Own spiritual family. That Bible truth is absolutely amazing.

You would think that believers would never lose sight of the fact that *even when they were spiritually "dead" in sin,* God raised them up, out of death into life and positioned them securely forever into Christ. But of course, this fact is what Satan wants us to forget, or to not understand, because the devil wants to block God's truth from taking root in our heart. That's why we must meditate on the Word of God, so that it sinks deep into our consciousness.

> Jesus said: *"When anyone hears the word of the kingdom, and does not understand it, then the wicked one comes and snatches away what was sown in his heart. This is he who received seed by the wayside."* Matthew 13:19

It's so important that we ask for God's wisdom in understanding the Bible, so that we will be victorious. *"Wisdom is the principal thing; therefore get wisdom: and with all your getting, get understanding." Proverbs 4:7.* Hearing the Word and not understanding it is like putting food in your mouth when your throat can't swallow anything; you could starve like that.

In the same way, "understanding" allows God's Word to sink down to penetrate our heart, where the Word is to germinate. It's vital for a speaker to expound the Word in such a way that it's easily understood. The Holy Spirit will quicken spiritual understanding to us, so that we can readily connect all the dots. You don't teach children different truth than you teach adults. You just need to do it on a different level, so that they can understand it.

I trust that this book is written to my reader's level of understanding, otherwise, the devil may snatch its message away. We all need God's wisdom and He assures us that we can freely ask for it. *"If any of you lacks wisdom, let him ask of God, who gives to all liberally and without reproach, and it will be given to you." James 1:5*

Being welcomed into God's family is awesome but there is even more good news. God gives His Holy Spirit as our continual living "guarantee" that we now belong to Him and not to the devil. *"Now He who establishes us with you in Christ and has anointed us, is God, who also has sealed us and given us the Spirit in our hearts as a guarantee." 2 Corinthians 1:21-22.*

This truth is confirmed again*: "having believed, you were sealed with the Holy Spirit of promise, who is the guarantee of our inheritance until the redemption of the purchased possession, to the praise of His glory."* Ephesians 1:13b-14

My Bible notes say: "The word "guarantee" in a business sense speaks of earnest money, a part of the purchase price paid in advance, as a down payment. It's the first installment, a pledge, or a deposit for planned future possession. In the Biblical sense, the word "guarantee" describes the Holy Spirit as the pledge of our future joys and bliss in Heaven. The Holy Spirit gives us a foretaste or guarantee of things to come."

To Satan, the above two verses must be like a "red flag" tormenting a bull. God has firmly claimed us for Himself, by placing His Own Spirit into our human spirit. Every time the devil looks at us, He can see God in our spirit; no wonder he hates us with a passion. In contrast, when the Father lovingly looks at us,

144

He forever sees us in our Heavenly position in Christ: He sees the Holy Spirit in us covering us with Christ's righteousness, even when we may see ourselves as a rotten sinner who fails miserably.

"Now He who has prepared us for this very thing is God, who also has given us the Spirit as a guarantee." 2 Corinthians 5:5. Because of his close walk with God, Paul saw his present earthly body as being a fragile temporary "tent" in contrast to his future eternal body. He had just said earlier in 2 Corinthians 5:1 *"For we know that if our earthly house, this tent, is destroyed, we have a building from God, a house not made with hands, eternal in Heaven."*

Satan really knows that he has no "genuine" authority over Christians, but that doesn't stop him from trying to rob them of the peace in knowing their inheritance in Christ. When a believer boldly refutes his lies, he has no other option but to temporarily back away until another situation presents itself for another attack.

How Satan must have hated Paul, no wonder he caused others to mistreat this saintly man. Paul totally understood His new Kingdom status and inheritance in God and wasn't overly concerned with the things of the world or even being attacked in his physical body. His one aim was to glorify the risen Lord and to teach others to do the same.

Because our human spirit longs to worship something, Satan is happy to fill that need in any way that suits the occasion. He leads people into false teaching about God, or he sidetracks our life so that we create our own god just so that we no longer feel empty in our spirit. We need to be aware that obsessions of any kind are useful tools that belong to the devil.

Unbelievers can have gods like fame, sport, riches, drugs, sex, philosophies, even education and business goals or perfecting the body beautiful. That's all okay with Satan. He is delighted if we worship anything except the One True God. He is cunning, creative and versatile. We can gullibly welcome "him" into our life as an angel of light, or we can fear him and his wicked representatives, like a roaring lion. Whether we are a believer or an unbeliever, Satan's intention is to always discredit the awesome goodness of God.

Many people have been innocently seduced into false belief systems when *"Satan transforms himself into an angel of light."* 2 *Corinthians 11:14.* My own grandmother comes to mind, but God saw her gentle kind heart and eventually she came to saving faith before she died. For most of her life, she had been truly seeking God but was led into the false teaching of the occult for fifty years, until she became a Christian a few years before she died at 96 years old.

Some people would not be taken in by an angel of light because they are not looking for any type of religious experience. Satan uses a different tactic. We are told: *"Be sober, be vigilant; because your adversary the devil walks about like a roaring lion, seeking whom he may devour."* 1 *Peter 5:8.* Satan is both a professional seducer and a brutal destroyer. He cannot tell the truth because Jesus said he was the father of all lies. (John 8:44)

We blatantly see Satan's work in society today. The media is full of horrible stories and these media reports are becoming increasingly scary. Violence is rapidly accelerating whilst the world's moral standards are declining alarmingly. Also, the gap between the rich and the poor is expanding. In today's society, "good" is called evil and "evil" is called good. Satan is having a field day, but I feel that His time is short. In the meantime, whatever "form" the devil takes, he is full of darkness, seeking only to destroy either by fear or by false peace.

Today, more than any time in history, it's absolutely vital that we, as believers, have sound biblical doctrine so that we are not deceived. Since our physical birth, Satan was our old slave-master right up to the moment of our salvation, but now that we are "in Christ," the devil is only a toothless tiger with a big roar.

Therefore, it is essential for us to walk in our Heavenly position in Christ and take back some of the territory he has tried to steal from us.

God has given us five weapons to use against Satan – the Word, the Name, the Blood, Praise and our personal Testimony. Any of these five weapons will make Satan severely tremble and squirm, so as to make him retreat or to backtrack for a short time.

- The Word: Obviously, to use the Word, we must first know it. Jesus used the Word against Satan in the wilderness. Jesus never wasted time arguing with him. On three occasions, Jesus simply quoted God's Word and the devil left him. Ephesians 6:17 calls the Bible the sword of the spirit. Hebrews 4:12 says the Bible is living and powerful and sharper than any two-edged sword. Satan hates the Bible.

- The Name: There is power in the Name of Jesus. As believers, we can command Satan to go in His Name – all demons have no other option but to depart. On earth, Jesus cast out demons; He had power over them and gave His power to His disciples who later went out and cast out demons themselves in Name of Jesus. We read in Luke 10:17 *"Then the seventy returned with joy saying, 'Lord, even the demons are subject to us in Your name.'"* Peter healed a lame man by the Name of Jesus in Acts 3:6

- The Blood: The Israelites were saved from slavery to the brutal Egyptians by the blood of a perfect lamb smeared on their door frame. After the resurrection, Jesus, our Great High Priest, presented His blood to His Father in Heaven, as the seal of reconciliation completed. Only then could the Holy Spirit be received by the believer. The blood and the Spirit are together linked as it is only through the blood of

147

Jesus that the Spirit can dwell in man. Believers are saved by the precious blood of God's Perfect Lamb – this is the work of Redemption. Also, it is only the blood of Jesus that has power to bring cleansing - 1 John 1:7, forgiveness and redemption - Colossians 1:14.

• Praising God: This is seen to be foolishness to the world, but it's the secret to victory for the Word says that *"God has chosen the foolish things of the world to put to shame the wise, and God has chosen the weak things of the world to put to shame the things which are mighty." 1 Corinthians 1:27.* God says about us: *"you are holy, enthroned in the praises of Israel." Psalm 22:3.* We can be confident that God inhabits the praise of His people today. In the Old Testament in 2 Chronicles 20:12, we read: *"When they began to sing and to praise, the Lord set ambushes against the (enemies) of Judah and they were defeated."* Praise is therefore the believer's battle banner. The Hebrew word for Praise is "halal," it means to thank, rejoice and to boast about someone. It conveys the idea or speaking or singing about the glories, virtues, or honor of someone. *Satan hates us praising God.*

• Personal Testimony: No one can dispute our testimony of the power of God in our life. Our testimony has three unique elements: (1) What our life was; (2) How we came to salvation: and (3) What our life is now like. *We know* that we are not the same person we once were, so no one can speak against a believer's salvation testimony.

Satan squirms when you say positive things about others, because he hates all forms of encouragement. Bad news on the media attracts the attention of most people far more than good news. In fact, it's totally normal to go about life and not have anyone say good things about you. Why not be refreshingly unique by making a positive difference in the lives of others, just by being aware of them in a nice way. For example, you can easily acknowledge people with a simple smile or a short greeting. This will make them feel appreciated and that's a good thing.

You don't have to have a great ministry or be a world-changer to make a positive impact in the lives of others. You can just encourage someone and make a big difference *to that person*. Ask God to make you conscious of the people around you, so that you may be able to make their day a little more pleasant. Too many believers are so preoccupied with their own agenda that they don't even notice those around them. If you are one of them, ask God to make you more sensitive to others. God never designed us to walk around with blinkers on.

Many people might be saying, "That's okay for you, Matthew, because you have the gift of encouragement." This is true, but I purposed in my heart years ago to make a conscious habit of looking at the faces of those who pass by me. Because of this gift, encouraging others comes naturally to me. Everyone has the ability to think of nice things to say about other people. It just takes a little bit of thought, that's all.

Think about who you can encourage now. Think of what you can honestly say about them that will lift them up. Be inspired by the fact that you will be making Satan squirm when you do so. The fact that Satan hates all encouragement may stimulate you into action more than anything else. You can start with a friend or a co-worker and branch out from there. Don't be afraid that people will make judgements about you, for if you speak from a pure heart, people won't see it as mere flattery.

Every single day all over the world, Satan kills people through accidents and diseases. If we have the ability to heal people, we would be able to thwart Satan's plans. Satan also destroys a Christian's faith in Jesus. In fact, many believers are now back in the world trying to forget the faith they once had. When we meet people like this, we can encourage them and share with them that Jesus still loves them.

I have met quite a number of people like this and have seen them cry after I ministered Jesus' love to them. Satan is especially annoyed when you minister to these people. They need to know that Jesus loves them despite their backsliding. They need to be lovingly restored into regular positive fellowship. They certainly don't need guilt in any form placed onto them.

Jesus told three parables, the Lost Sheep, the Lost Coin, and the Lost Son, in Luke Chapter 15. All three parables speak about the Father's joy when someone or something is lovingly restored back to the right place. If you are ever given the opportunity to minister and talk with a person who once embraced Christianity, ask if you can pray for them and ask the Lord to lead them back home in His time. God loves all lost believers so it's very important to let them know that you too care about them. Tell them that they are certainly not lost to God and His heart longs for them to come back into close fellowship.

People leave the faith for all sorts of reasons, but we can be sure that Satan has thrown out some kind of "bait of offence" to them and instead of letting it fall to the ground, the person has picked it up, so "offence" immediately begins to do its negative work in that person's heart. You could be the one who lovingly restores such a person's focus back onto Jesus and remind them that their real enemy is Satan and not the person who has been his mouthpiece.

The Word of God tells us who our real enemies are: *"We do not wrestle against flesh and blood, but against principalities, against powers, against the rulers of the darkness of this age, against spiritual hosts of wickedness in Heavenly places."* Ephesians 6:12

Other humans are not our enemy because God created mankind in His Own image. However, people ignorantly pick up one of Satan's rotten baits of "offense" and in doing so, they have caused harm to themself and to others. An excellent book to read on this subject, or to even do a Bible Study on is "The Bait of Satan" by John Bevere.

If Jesus gives you an opportunity to talk to a back-slider, encourage them. Try not to put pressure on them, but be outwardly positive and loving towards them, while inwardly praying for their full restoration back into fellowship. The world is lost outside of Jesus. Most of us have plenty of opportunities every day to be a light to the world. Take advantage of these opportunities by giving people a positive experience when they encounter you. We are to never under-estimate the life-changing power of the Holy Spirit living within us.

Satan has the vast majority of people in the world blinded to the truth of Jesus. Therefore, it is time for believers to be God's light to those we meet and shine forth hope and the brilliance of Christ to others. When we shine, this makes Satan squirm. I believe that it will not be long before the second return of Christ as evil is rapidly escalating everywhere around us and Biblical prophecy must come to pass.

"You are of God, little children, and have overcome them, because He who is in you is greater than he who is in the world." 1 John 4:4

Satan has some people believing that he is as powerful as God, or at least he is more powerful than Michael the archangel. This is one of the lies that he has brought into the church. But one day, Michael is going to put Satan into chains. And then later on, he is going to throw Satan into the eternal lake of fire.

The world is in such a mess and often, we give our enemy more credit than he deserves. Yes, he is *like* a roaring lion seeking whom he can devour, but he is utterly toothless, meaning, he can only really "gum" a believer, as Jesus has forever defeated Him on the cross. Sometimes, believers forget that they have the awesome power of the Holy Spirit of God dwelling in them and we forget that the One in us is so much greater than Satan. (1 John 4:4b)

Every believer can make this deceiving scumbag squirm, by knowing who they are spiritually and by overcoming him by any of the five points listed earlier in this chapter. Any of these weapons will cause Satan or his demons to take flight. The indwelling Holy Spirit gives us the authority to use these weapons against all his attacks on us, or our loved ones and those we pray for in the world.

Satan's hatred for all humanity is intense! Never lose sight of the fact that Satan thrives on destroying everything that God loves and he wants to fill our lives with everything God hates.

Believers can make Satan squirm by bringing life to people with prophetic or healing words, or by doing encouraging acts of kindness in a person's life. Kindness towards others has eternal rewards and as your heart flows with the love of Jesus, you become a powerful weapon for God to use against the devices of the enemy.

Here in Sydney, Australia, there are so many people needing help; you only need to go out of your home to see a homeless person. These down-trodden people can do with a friendly greeting. Perhaps, there are people who are not doing well in your local church. Befriend them, for this will bring some light into their life. Inviting them home for a simple meal or even for a coffee tells them that you care and it's really an easy thing to do. If you ask Jesus to open your eyes to people in need, He will do this because it is part of His plan for your life.

Helping people by being Christ to them will assure you or many rewards in eternity.

CHAPTER 19
VICTORIOUS LIVING

Living the Christian life is a continual challenge. Conquering fear, overcoming sin, and walking in holiness is difficult, as it goes against our fleshly desires. Holiness has been a definite challenge to me for as I have said, I still struggle with certain things.

We all have a common enemy who keeps coming against us in our weak spots. We therefore, need to agree with the conclusions made by the Apostle Paul, who had himself been tested in his faith at *every* point. After writing so many glorious truths about our "standing in Christ" in Romans Chapter 8, he summed up with his final victorious conclusion: *"What then shall we say to these things? If God is for us, who can be against us?" Romans 8:31*

When I think about it, no matter who has risen up against me, I still go on and do what the Lord has for me. God knows what He wants to achieve in my life and He has promised to complete the work He has began. (Philippians 1:6) No one can really stand in the way of that being accomplished, except of course our own will. Sure, people can rise up in opposition to us, but down the road in life, we can look back and we can see that they were just small speed bumps on the road to victory. In fact, what Satan means for evil, God uses these speed bumps to refine us and to make us more determined and resolved to do the will of God.

God is on our side, so what can man really do to us to thwart His plans in our life? One of the keys to a victorious Christian life is to know what you are here to do on earth and start to do it. God will help you in this. He will also help you to keep on track, so that you do it.

Some people might be convinced that a particular sin is going to keep them out of Heaven. I struggled with this belief for most of my Christian life and the thoughts only abated when I saw my mansion in Heaven made up of all the things I love. Many people think they simply are not going to be able to make it to Heaven. This passage has been comforting to me.

> *"Yet in all these things we are more than conquerors through Him who loved us. For I am persuaded that neither death nor life, nor angels nor principalities nor powers, nor things present nor things to come, nor height nor depth, nor any other created thing, shall be able to separate us from the love of God which is in Christ Jesus our Lord."* Romans 8:37-39

Like Paul, we too, can be confident of these things. A conqueror fights the enemy and wins the battle. The good thing is that *we didn't even do the fighting, Jesus did it for us!* In God's sight, the battle against Satan is over and Jesus won it for us over two thousand years ago. All that is left for us to do is to humbly receive the benefits just like the Israelites bought home the spoil from their enemies thousands of years ago. To my mind, that's certainly being more than a conqueror.

Nothing can stop God loving you. Not demons; not death; not any created thing because you are forever in His mind: *"Can a woman forget her nursing child, and not have compassion on the son of her womb? Yet, I will not forget you. See, I have inscribed you on the palms of My hand."* Isaiah 49:15-16.

It is not natural for a parent to abandon their own child, but it has happened because we live in a fallen world. But God is from a far higher dimension, His ways are perfect and He will never abandon His Own children. Nor can He possibly forget us because He has our names forever with Him. We are His trophy and prized masterpiece.

Although we may feel at times that God has forgotten us because we have allowed sin to pull us away from Him, we are to take comfort that we are continually on His mind. We, at times, do pull away, but it's never the other way around. Because of God's promises and His covenant keeping nature, as well as His precious Holy Spirit living in us, God will keep us and bring us into Heaven with His love. Knowing that we are loved, forgiven, and justified is so reassuring. Jesus has not only promised to care for us on life's current journey but He will care for us throughout all eternity.

If your life is continually plagued with guilt, shame and condemnation over things you regret doing, confess them to God and move on with His forgiveness and grace. God wants us to live a victorious Christian life. Allowing shame to rob us of God's peace, only gives Satan a secure foot-hold to have his way in us. We need to know the truth and to stand on the truth for us to be live free of guilt. When Jesus was interceding to His Father for us, the night before He died, He said: *"Sanctify them by Your truth, Your word is truth." John 17:17*

The Bible is the written Word and Jesus is the living Word of God. Jesus said that He was the "way" to God the Father, because He was God's "truth" and He alone was "eternal life." Also we learn that the: *"law was given through Moses, but grace and truth came through Jesus Christ." John 1:17.* The Law preserved God's people until the cross of Jesus. Now it is Jesus who will preserve, protect and take us into the loving arms of our Father in Heaven.

For many years, I meditated on Psalm Chapter 1: 1-3. *"Oh, the joys of those who do not follow the advice of the wicked, or stand around with sinners, or join in with mockers. But they delight in the law of the Lord, meditating on it day and night. They are like trees planted along the riverbank, bearing fruit each season. Their leaves never wither, and they prosper in all they do." Psalm 1:1-3 (New Living Translation)*

Early in our Christian life, we are to purposely distance ourselves from people who boast of their sinful lifestyle and those who mock our faith. Many sinners are focused on spending their days gossiping and chasing the pleasures of the world. As we continually seek the Lord with all our heart, we will have abundant joy and all that we do will prosper. As we mature, God wants us to pray specifically for those who know Him not and to be His ambassadors to do our part in the reconciliation work of God in a sinner's life. *"For there is one God and one Mediator between God and men, the Man Christ Jesus." 1 Timothy 2:5*

My Testimony: For many years, I studied this verse and meditated on it. I found that to obey this verse, I had to leave some of my best friends behind. I had to choose to have no friends rather than have the wrong ones.

Now, I am happy to say that many things that I am turning my hands to are prospering. My books are going well. My Facebook group, "Open Heavens and Intimacy with Jesus" is going well and many people are joining and interacting with each other. I have started a course called the "School of the Prophets" on Skype and that is doing really well. Every time I write a book, the Holy Spirit gives me a title and chapter headings for it. I find that by the time one book is published, I have another one already written. I always looked forward to a day when all I did was prospering and that day has come for me.

I am a tree who is planted next to the river drawing the Holy Spirit up into my roots. I have spiritual fruit which is helping people believe in Jesus. Though I sometimes suffer with depression, I believe that God is still using me powerfully. Even in the midst of depression, the Lord can still cause me to be bright and to encourage people. Every day, my books are being downloaded and helping people. In that way, my leaves are green and not withering.

We all need to constantly choose who we will trust and follow. Will we follow what comes natural to our flesh? Or will we follow the teachings of Jesus and the leadings of the Holy Spirit? If we choose to follow the ways of God, then these verses come true in our life:

"Blessed is the man who trusts in the Lord, and whose hope is the Lord. For he shall be like a tree planted by the waters, which spreads out its roots by the river, and will not fear when heat comes; But its leaf will be green, and will not be anxious in the year of drought, nor will it cease from yielding fruit." Jeremiah 17:7-8

Once again, a person in God's will is compared to a tree by the waters. This time, the tree does not cease from bearing fruit. In addition, this person will not become anxious in the year of drought. When hard times come to this person, they will remain in God's peace and will be assured that the Lord will look after them. Wouldn't that be a wonderful way to live? Would you like to be a tree like this that bore fruit for other people to eat?

Would you like to live a victorious life? The key to doing this is by trusting in the Lord and following His ways.

It was close to twenty years between when I first read the above Old Testament verses and when I started to live them out and see everything that I do, prosper! I am not saying it will take twenty years for you, I know that many people will grasp and walk in this easier than I did. We need to be able to trust in the Lord. David says this: *"Commit your way to the Lord, trust also in Him, and He shall bring it to pass. He shall bring forth your righteousness as the light, and your justice as the noonday."* Psalm 37:5-6

This is a precious promise. Wouldn't you like to see your desires and dreams come to pass? It may sound simple, but we need to commit our dreams to the Lord and trust in Him alone and this passage says that God will bring it to pass. What could be more victorious, than for your dreams and desires in this life to come to pass?

"The Lord will perfect that which concerns me." Psalm 138a. If you are praying for someone you love to be saved, claim this verse continually. It was the verse that my mother claimed for her mother for over thirty years before it came to pass. There may be something other than salvation, that you earnestly desire and you are sure that it would be God's will - you can also claim this verse.

Be confident that God's word will not return to Him void. (Isaiah 55:11) He has invited us to call out to Him, His telephone number is triple three, for He says: *"Call to Me, and I will answer you, and show you great and mighty things, which you do not know." Jeremiah 33:3*

How would you like God to boast when it came to you? How would you like your sense of justice seeing the light of day? This is a heritage of the saints of God. If we look up to God; walk in the Holy Spirit and trust God we can do great things. We can not only make an impact in this earthly realm but in Heaven itself. The Lord your God *"will rejoice over you with gladness, He will quiet you with His love, He will rejoice over you with singing." Zephaniah 3:17.* Can you see the Lord God Almighty dancing for joy over you?

CHAPTER 20
"WELL DONE, GOOD AND FAITHFUL SERVANT"

We each have been given just one life and we have all been given unique talents. We have gone on a journey of discovery in this book and seeing that you are at the last chapter, I presume that you have been with me from the very beginning.

Our Master has gone to a far country. As well as giving us our life, our talents and many golden opportunities, God has allowed us to become members of His own family, but just like Jesus was God's obedient Servant on earth, so too, He wants us to be His obedient servants and stewards. This not only brings joy to the Father, but it will also bring joy to us.

Jesus said that some of us were given five talents: having much ability and a lot of gifting. Some of us were more average and were given two talents, while some received just one talent. We know that all believers are going to be judged one day by how we have invested the things that God has entrusted to us. (See my Chapter 2 and 1 Corinthians 3:12-15)

It is my earnest hope that throughout this book, I have encouraged you to live a life that will see you invest it wisely in self denial. I hope that you will lay up for yourself Heavenly treasures so that one day, our Master Jesus will say, "Well done, good and faithful servant. Enter into the joy of your Lord."

"For the kingdom of Heaven is like a man travelling to a far country, who called his own servants and delivered his goods to them. And to one he gave five talents, to another two, and to another one, to each according to his own ability; and immediately he went on a journey. Then he who had received the five talents

went and traded with them, and made another five talents. And likewise he who had received two gained two more also. But he who had received one went and dug in the ground, and hid his lord's money. After a long time the lord of those servants came and settled accounts with them.

"So he who had received five talents came and brought five other talents, saying, 'Lord, you delivered to me five talents; look, I have gained five more talents besides them.' His lord said to him, 'Well done, good and faithful servant; you were faithful over a few things, I will make you ruler over many things. Enter into the joy of your lord.' He also who had received two talents came and said, 'Lord, you delivered to me two talents; look, I have gained two more talents besides them.' His lord said to him, 'Well done, good and faithful servant; you have been faithful over a few things, I will make you ruler over many things. Enter into the joy of your lord.'

"Then he who had received the one talent came and said, 'Lord, I knew you to be a hard man, reaping where you have not sown, and gathering where you have not scattered seed. And I was afraid, and went and hid your talent in the ground. Look, there you have what is yours.'

"But his lord answered and said to him, 'You wicked and lazy servant, you knew that I reap where I have not sown, and gather where I have not scattered seed. So you ought to have deposited my money with the bankers, and at my coming I would have received back my own with interest. Therefore take the talent from him, and give it to him who has ten talents.

"For to everyone who has, more will be given, and he will have abundance; but from him who does not have, even what he has will be taken away. And cast the unprofitable servant into the outer darkness. There will be weeping and gnashing of teeth." Matthew 25:14-30

I have done my best to encourage you. I have gone over what I have written about four times and done partial editing and some rewriting. My manuscript will go now to my mother to edit and then another editor to copy edit and proof read. At the end of it, I will re-read everything and perhaps make minor changes. Then all that I have said will be in your hands.

My question to you is this: Are you going to live the same way that you were living before reading this book, or are you going to make some changes? Are you going to re-read some of the chapters? I trust that you will buy at least some of the books I have suggested and read them also. Are you going to discover what you are born for? Are you going to train and learn to hear Jesus speak? Or is this book just going to be a book you read and don't apply?

I pray that you are encouraged and you go on to do great things with your life and you store up plenty of treasures in Heaven. I know one day, I will meet you in glory and we can have a great conversation together.

I'd love to hear from you

One way that you can let me know that you loved my book is to take five minutes of your time and write an honest review of this book on Amazon. Many people search Amazon for reviews before they buy a book an your review of this book is a simple way to let people know it is worth their time to read it. This is one way that you an sow into my ministry that will really bless me and others.

You can write to me at survivors.sanctuary@gmail.com

You can sow money into my book producing ministry at
http://personal-prophecy-today.com

I'd love to hear from you

Matthew Robert Payne

September 2015

OTHER BOOKS BY MATTHEW ROBERT PAYNE

The Parables of Jesus Made Simple

The Prophetic Supernatural Experience

Prophetic Evangelism Made Simple

Kingdom Nuggets

You Identity in Christ

His Redeeming Love- A Memoir

Great Cloud of Witnesses Speak

Writing and Self Publishing Christian Nonfition

Coping with your pain and Suffering

You can find all these books at this link
http://tinyurl.com/nms9evz

www.ingramcontent.com/pod-product-compliance
Lightning Source LLC
Chambersburg PA
CBHW021844090426
42811CB00033B/2139/J